In Search of a Full Life

In Search of a **Full Life**

A Practical and Spiritual Guide

Leonard J. DeLorenzo

Our Sunday Visitor
Huntington, Indiana

Nihil Obstat
Msgr. Michael Heintz, Ph.D.
Censor Librorum

Imprimatur
✠ Kevin C. Rhoades
Bishop of Fort Wayne-South Bend
August 31, 2023

The *Nihil Obstat* and *Imprimatur* are official declarations that a book is free from doctrinal or moral error. It is not implied that those who have granted the *Nihil Obstat* and *Imprimatur* agree with the contents, opinions, or statements expressed.

Scripture texts in this work are taken from the *Revised Standard Version of the Bible*—Second Catholic Edition (Ignatius Edition) Copyright © 2006 National Council of the Churches of Christ in the United States of America. Used by permission. All rights reserved worldwide.

Scripture texts marked "JPS" are taken from *The Jewish Study Bible*, Jewish Publication Society, TANAKH Translation © 1985, 1999, published by Oxford University Press © 2004.

Every reasonable effort has been made to determine copyright holders of excerpted materials and to secure permissions as needed. If any copyrighted materials have been inadvertently used in this work without proper credit being given in one form or another, please notify Our Sunday Visitor in writing so that future printings of this work may be corrected accordingly.

Our Sunday Visitor Publishing Division
Our Sunday Visitor, Inc.
200 Noll Plaza
Huntington, IN 46750
www.osv.com
1-800-348-2440

ISBN: 978-1-63966-067-4 (Inventory No. T2809)
1. RELIGION—Christian Living—Personal Growth.
2. RELIGION—Christian Living—Spiritual Growth.
3. RELIGION—Christianity—Catholic.
eISBN: 978-1-63966-068-1

LCCN: 2023947590

Cover design: Tyler Ottinger
Interior design: Amanda Falk
Cover art: AdobeStock

PRINTED IN THE UNITED STATES OF AMERICA

To our godsons:
Tommy, Marty, and James

Contents

1

How to Be Real

We do not know each other, and yet I count you as a friend. Why? Because I have affection for you, I care about your well-being, and I will your good.

I write to you not from a position of perfect knowledge or absolute certainty, but from a heart that empathizes with you on account of the challenges you face and lack of clarity often offered to you. I have been where you are, though in a different generation and under different circumstances. I was guided into a more full and meaningful Catholic life through timely mentoring, the good fortune of substantive faith communities, and good religious education. And yet I was far from always intentional in seeking out a mature Catholic life, and those who formed me were not always committed to that end, either. I want more for you than there was for me, and I want you to become more confident, more open, more creative, and more real than I myself have yet become. I don't write to you so that you can become like me. I write to you so that you can become truly yourself, as you were created and are called to become.

I don't assume you are a committed Catholic. Perhaps you were baptized and even completed your initiation into the Catholic Church through First Communion and Confirmation, and yet you don't think of yourself as "Catholic" first of all. It may be something in the background for you, like the state or town in which you happened to be born. You might consider it to be something more about your past — or your parents' or grandparents' past — than about your future. You might be angry, frustrated, or, frankly, just bored with the Church, and I get all of that. I've been there, and sometimes I'm still there.

You also might not be Catholic. Maybe you are interested in the Catholic Faith, and you are poking around for insight or wisdom. Maybe you were in the Church but you left the Church, and somehow this book made its way to you. Or maybe you are not quite sure what to think about yourself, but this "Catholic thing" seems like it might be part of the equation, even if only as something to figure out or get over.

Then again, maybe you are a committed Catholic, or even consider yourself "very committed." You would like to truly live as if you were "in the world but not of the world," and yet trying to figure out how to be faithful and genuine and even a little imperfect is tough. Maybe you are really invested in being *fully* Catholic but also, at the same time, fully at ease with others and persuasive to others who are not as "all in" as you currently are.

I don't begin by creating my own image of you, as if expecting you to fit what I imagine. I want to write to you as you are and speak to you as a friend. That means I will speak honestly. I want to tell you the truth and help you find the fullness of life.

I believe I know what it means to become a mature and committed Catholic. That doesn't mean I myself have become the kind of mature and committed Catholic I hope to be. Rather, I've come to understand what a mature and committed Catholic is through my studies, in certain people I've spent time with, and even by the as yet unfulfilled longings in my own practice of the Faith. I want to provide you real and meaningful assistance in how to become a mature and committed Catholic.

Of course, I cannot force you to follow this path — nor would I ever want to force you — but I am absolutely determined to empower you. *If* you want to seek this end, then I want to give you the means for doing so. I am titling each chapter with "How to" to keep me honest and on task: I intend for everything you read here to be practical and to offer you real guidance on the way to something of significance and consequence.

Getting Real

That brings me to the first matter at hand: how to be real. We start here because everything to follow depends on being real, not fake; honest, not deceptive; practical *and* spiritual. To be real means to take responsibility for becoming someone of definite character. Your character is the result of the commitments and sacrifices you make, as well as the foundation for the kind of person you become in the future. We live in an environment that does not make developing substantive character easy or likely to happen. It is easier to be something like a shape-shifter, more comfortable with changing who you appear to be in response to passing fads or social expectations.

Think about it: What tends to be valued in our world today is becoming a bundle of reactions. You are expected to react to everything, to have a "hot take," to always have to have a fully formulated view without any time to really formulate one. We hear something, and we are expected to react quickly and strongly, as through social media. One political movement is shown to be corrupt and another comes promising liberation, and we are to react by condemning one and hailing the other, only to go through the same cycle next time around with new movements. One fashion wanes and some new one emerges, and we must react by adapting our tastes. Schools or employers change what they value for admissions or hiring, and we react by changing what we value as good and worthy of pursuit.

When I speak of "being real," I do not mean to suggest that the point is to become static, inflexible, and stubborn. What I mean is that being real is being free from the rapid and sudden changes around us; it means being able to deal with these changes honestly and to actually lead others toward a vision of what is true, valuable, and worthy of pursuit — in season and out of season.

How do you become real and thus capable of taking responsibility for becoming someone of definite character? You engage in small, specific, definite practices. At the risk of oversimplifying, you focus on developing certain habits. That is precisely what I write about in this book. Your intentions are very important; it matters what kind of person you *hope* to become. But intentions dissipate unless they become incarnate through repeatable actions. I use the word *incarnate* purposefully. I mean that through the kind of practices we will focus on in these pages, we slowly become who we are meant to be. Intention and desire become flesh.

You and I both know how unstable our lives and even the whole world can become in the blink of an eye — if the COVID-19 pandemic taught us anything, it taught us that. The antidote to that instability is to develop and grow from stable practices that lead us toward taking responsibility for becoming someone of definite character. The fullness of life that Jesus Christ promises is about becoming more and more ourselves, as we were created to be and are now called to become. Who you are and who you become matter, absolutely.

What matters is becoming who we are created to be rather than *appearing* to be something. None of us likes it when we feel that someone is being inauthentic or disingenuous. It is far better if people are honest about their faults and show themselves to be incomplete, rather than pretending to be something they're not. We don't want that from others, and if we're honest, we don't want that for ourselves either. I want you to give yourself permission to be "in process"; to not have it all together yet; to be able to struggle and strive and fail; and to be honest about it all. At the same time, though, I want you to feel challenged to move toward the definite end of becoming a person fully capable of commitment, sacrifice, and joy. When we are capable of those things, then we are *really* real — not as someone else, but as our true selves.

2

How to Listen

We are surrounded by so much noise that it is impossible to listen. Seems counterintuitive, doesn't it? We might think that since there is so much to hear we would be listening all the time. But most of the time, we are listening in the same way that someone who is drowning is drinking: We are taking in so much that rather than refreshing us, the noise is swallowing us up.

Your attention is a limited resource and, like every limited resource, it is precious. It is so precious that, at every moment of every day, people and companies that you do not know are bidding against each other, with actual money, to occupy your attention. Look at this, listen to this, think about this — now quick, over here, now over there.

You know what I am talking about, right? It's like standing in a room when suddenly voices and other sounds come so quickly from every direction that you spin around to face one only to hear another right away and spin again. Your attention is limited, but the competition for it is so fierce that you often feel overwhelmed.

Here's the problem: We are constantly trying to pay attention to so many things that we rarely pay close attention to anything. Think about that phrase "pay attention." We "pay" because attention costs us. But since we are surrounded by so much noise, we usually find ourselves nearly broke. There is little if anything in the bank, and our credit is maxed out. We don't have any attention to "pay" because it has all been spent — or, rather, it has been taken from us. That means that whatever or whoever happens to be right in front of us right now receives very little attention. We just don't have any to give; our attention is spread so widely that there is little left to spend in the here and now.

I cannot describe for you exactly what this is like in your life, but I suspect you know the feeling of being stretched and pulled, inundated and overwhelmed by oh-so-many things. You must know what it is like to glance and glance again at one thing after another as sounds and images scroll by or surround you. I bet you know the strange sensation of being somewhere but not really being there because your attention is scattered across so many other places. I suspect you, like me, know what it is like to hear much but listen to little.

It is important that we talk about listening here at the outset, because nothing else will matter if we do not learn how to listen. We could talk about prayer and studying, being mentored and being uncomfortable, or even reading Scripture and becoming Eucharistic, but if we do not work together on learning how to listen, none of that is likely to go anywhere. Because here is the rock-bottom truth: When we are submerged in noise, we are not free. We cannot be fully human if we are not free, and the mature Catholic life is all about freedom — true freedom.

Learning how to listen is about becoming free to give and invest your attention. You are not free to "pay attention" when your attention is being taken from you by people and groups you barely know who are competing for it. This might sound dramatic, but I am not being dramatic enough. What takes up your attention inevitably influences and shapes you. This is an unalterable fact about us as human beings. What we can decide is who and what has the privilege of influencing and shaping us. That requires developing the discipline and power to guard your attention against the innumerable forces competing for it. Later on we will think about and learn how to practice giving our attention to those who matter most — family and friends, those in need, even God — but for now we want to focus on becoming better stewards of our attention by learning how to listen better.

Practicing Attention

As I said before, having the right intentions matters, but intention alone is not enough. What we need are small, specific, definite practices that allow our intentions to become incarnate, to become more than ideas or theories. Practices shape who we are. I therefore offer you three specific practices to allow the intention of learning how to listen to slowly take hold in your life.

First, take time every single day to remove yourself from the noise. Rather than an abstract goal, this must be a firm and definite commitment. Choose fifteen minutes at the same time every day and dedicate that time to just being alone, in silence. Write this time in dark, permanent ink on your daily schedule. Make this nonnegotiable. Prepare for this time every day by removing the things that would distract you. Lock away your phone. Turn off notifications. Go to a private place. Set a timer so you are not tempted to look at the clock. Then just allow yourself to be present in this time, attentive but not distracted. What matters is that you do this every day. Later, we will talk about how to unite this particular practice to prayer and to attend to God, but before that, we have to work on reclaiming our power of attention from all the many things that steal it away.

Second, set aside one day a week to refrain from being plugged-in and working. Because we have the means for always being connected, every day ends up being the same in terms of thinking and worrying about the same things. For one day a week, break the cycle.

Ideally, this day will be Sunday, the Christian Sabbath. Plan to spend this day differently. Spend time with the people around you without checking on what's going on with other people in other places. Read. Rest. Cultivate your hobbies. Serve someone who needs help. I am under no illusion here: This is a difficult and costly commitment. In order to dedicate this one day, you will need to be more focused and disciplined the other six days of the week, because you will need to accomplish your work during those six days in order to free up this one day. Plan accordingly.

Third and finally, resist the urge to fill in the in-between times. These are times like when you are standing in line, stuck in traffic, or waiting for someone to arrive. What do most of us do in times like these? We grab our phones and quickly scroll or check in or browse around. That might not seem like a big deal, but the cumulative effect of all these little in-between moments is that we become less and less capable of just waiting and being bored. We lose sight of what and who might actually be around us in times like these. We let other things and influences steal our attention in small doses, and we quickly become dependent on — or even addicted to — that habit. We soon do this without thinking about it. That's not freedom. So the practice for reclaiming the freedom we lose is to willfully resist the urge to fill in the in-between times. No doubt, you will fail at this. The important thing is to keep trying. When you realize you gave in without thinking about it during an in-between time, just stop, lightly slap the back of your hand (or something like that), and put the phone away.

These three practices are simple and direct; they are also demanding. It will be difficult to allow these to become habitual. There is no shortcut here: The only thing to do is make the commitments and then work on keeping them. When you fail, try again. Work on these for a solid month, then spend some time assessing how your previous month was in terms of holding to these commitments and growing in attention. Are there things you would like to change or do differently? Have these practices improved your life in some way? If so, make the changes you want to make and then renew your commitment to these practices for another month.

3

How to Study and Work

Your value is measured according to how many things you can do at once. The key to being fully alive, maximally successful, and highly important is the ability to occupy yourself with as many things as possible, simultaneously. You are made to switch between tasks with increasing rapidity, all the way to the point of instantaneity. You are only as good as the number of things that you can do.

Everything you read in that first paragraph is a lie, and now I will stop lying to you. Neither of us is so naive as to think that anyone tells us lies like these outright.

No one has to. If we reflect on what we have subconsciously assumed about what qualifies as impressive or winning or even thriving, we might recognize that this elusive image of a person who does many, many things at once — and seemingly does it all with ease — is silently held up as the ideal. When we do not live up to that silent expectation, we often feel empty, resentful, or angry.

When we manage for a brief time to do it all, we feel fulfilled, but the feeling is fleeting. This ideal is not only impossible to achieve and sustain, it is also diabolical. It is born of a spirit that will lead us to despair, one that insists that the human being fully alive is the one who is "always doing everything."

This is the myth of multitasking. You and I never took a class on multitasking — we have simply assumed its value and learned how to multitask through practice. If you are like me, it is hard to resist multitasking. Just doing one thing at a time never feels like enough.

The myth that multitasking brings us to fulfillment is bolstered by innumerable images of presumed success that surround us, but perhaps the very worst part is that the myth is strengthened by what emerges within us. When we multitask, we think that we are getting better and better at paying attention to every single thing we are managing. But the truth is that the more we multitask, the *worse* we get at paying close attention to any single thing we manage. The appearance and the reality are out of whack. It is all a myth.

Multitasking changes the kind of person you are and what you are capable of; just as, on the other side, the habit of focused and singular attentiveness changes you. Clifford Nass was a communications professor at Stanford who studied the effects of multitasking, and he came to a pretty decisive conclusion from what he saw when he studied people who multitask:

> So we have scales that allow us to divide up people into people who multitask all the time and people who rarely do, and the differences are remarkable. People who multitask all the time can't filter out irrelevancy. They can't manage a working memory. They're chronically distracted. They initiate larger parts of their brain that are irrelevant to the task at hand … they're pretty much mental wrecks. … Unfortunately, they've developed habits of mind that make it impossible for them to be laser-focused. They're suckers for irrelevancy. They just can't keep on task.[1]

This is the lie I'm talking about. We think we are really good at multitasking and that we can shift gears to being hyperfocused when we need to be, but the truth is that by continually multitasking, we lose the ability to focus. We cannot focus well even when we want to. "Always doing everything" leads to "never doing anything well."

Reclaiming Focus

I want you to know about this because the way you study and the way you work change the kind of person you will become. The content of study and work is important, but so is the manner in which we study and work. Developing healthy and life-giving habits of study and work requires intentionality and repetition. Multitasking has become the default, so we need to work hard to create a new normal. I want to share with you three recommendations for how to study and work well.

First, set aside time for your study and work. It typically takes about ninety minutes of continuous attention to develop insights and reap some of the fruits of true concentration, accounting for the time it takes to settle in and get your bearings with a task or project.[2] That might sound like a long time — and at first, it is — but with practice, we become more and more accustomed to concentrating for longer periods of time. At first — if you do not already do this — plan to give thirty minutes of uninterrupted attention to what you need to work on or study. Then give yourself a break, before returning for another thirty minutes. After a week or so, try to increase your blocks of concentration to forty-five minutes, then sixty, up to ninety minutes. One of the secondary benefits you will soon discover is that you are a lot more efficient with your time, while the quality of your work also increases.

Second, prepare a space for your study and work, and clear out distractions. You and I both know that if your phone is next to you, you are going to check it. We know that if our sports channel, favorite news site, or social media page is open, we are going to constantly peek. And we know that if we put ourselves in an environment with other things that will distract us — friends, TVs, etc. — we will be swayed to break concentration again and again. So choose your spot(s) well. Or, if you have an assigned place of work for your job, think ahead to how you can organize that space to help you stay on your chosen task. The other part of preparation is the importance of planning breaks. Maybe there is some mindless game you like playing — OK, plan to play that for ten minutes after one of your blocks of concentration. In other words, contain what would otherwise become a distraction. Give it its own time and space, which is separate from the time and space for concentration.

Third, use a timer. Checking a clock is another form of distraction, leading to a strange kind of multitasking where you are keeping track of time in addition to whatever else you are doing. So just set a timer with an alarm, then forget about the time. Just focus on what you are doing. Free yourself from the burden of keeping track of time.

These are practical strategies that put us on course to avoid being mental wrecks, as habitual multitaskers are proven to be, moving us instead toward becoming more of what we, as human beings, are meant to be. We are meant to use our minds to dig into the depths of things. We are meant to develop the skills in our bodies to become more and more expert at our crafts. And above all, we are meant to be able to give our focus and attention to what (and especially to whom) is right in front of us, being fully present rather than chronically partially present. As we will explore later, this is all part of training for intimacy, which requires heartfelt attentiveness.

You might be protesting along the lines of, "Well, a great chef multitasks, paying attention to lots of things all at once." Or we might imagine an air traffic controller, an orchestra conductor, or a parent. Indeed, each of these persons deals with increasing levels of complexity, but the ones who have developed expertise are wholly focused and present to what they are doing. The great chef is not also writing a sonnet, tracking a ballgame, and texting. Air traffic controllers do not work on crossword puzzles while directing aircraft. Likewise, the focused and present parent is not the one who checks work email while with his kids, but rather gives his undivided attention to the variety of things going on with his children at a given time.

A friend of mine who is an expert woodworker once said in an interview that, while in the shop, "I'm always in a state of focused attention. First of all, you're trying not to cut your thumbs off. You're always focused on that." Indeed. I learned something like this when I waited tables at a steakhouse. As a waiter, I had a lot of people to serve and myriad little details to attend to.

But I was at my best when I was focused on that work, not splitting my focus on other things at the same time. There was a kind of mastery in being fully present to the work at hand, which required keeping distractions at bay with intentional breaks.

Much of what I talked about here and in the previous chapter will find resonances in the next three chapters, which will explore how to pray. I did not address prayer first because I wanted to spend time helping you think about these more natural abilities we develop for listening and for study or work, because prayer has to do with spiritual abilities, and those spiritual abilities build on natural abilities. Attention, focus, concentration, and presence are the natural abilities that God's grace builds on and perfects when we seek him in prayer.

4

How to Pray — Part 1

You will often hear people tell you to think of prayer as a relationship. Do not do that. At least, do not start from there. Beginning by thinking of prayer as a relationship will inevitably lead you to think of this "relationship" as comparable to other relationships.

In fact, without meaning to, you will bring your ideas about what a relationship should be to prayer, which means that you will hold God to your expectations. The truth of prayer is that it is *not* a relationship among equals. To the extent that prayer is a relationship, it is a relationship between you as a creature and your God who created you. The terms are not equal — they are anything but equal.

I'm placing a lot of emphasis on this one point in this first chapter on prayer. I know I run the risk of making prayer sound unattractive and thus losing your interest. I do want to appeal to you, but most of all I want to tell you the truth, and I think the idea of prayer as "relationship" gets in the way.

I should think about softening my point now, but, perhaps foolishly, I will not. To the contrary, I am going to press my point even further. I will do that by sharing with you what St. Catherine of Siena discovered about herself and God through her encounters with God in prayer. Her encounters became so vivid and so full that she often heard God speaking to her very directly, so much so that when she wrote about prayer, she routinely wrote in God's own voice. The following is what she wrote about the fundamental truth about herself in relation to God, written here in God's voice: "Do you not know, dear daughter, who you are and who I am? If you will know these two things you will be blessed. You are the one who is not, while I am He who is."[1]

That doesn't sound right, does it? We are supposed to believe in ourselves, trust in ourselves, and become convinced that we are enough just as we are. Yet here God says, "You are the one who is *not!*" Isn't that what all the marketers want us to think? That we are *not* enough, that we are *not* fulfilled, that we are *not* complete, so we need something to make us whole or better. Yes, that is what marketers want us to think. And yes, God says to Catherine in prayer: *You are not.*

But here is the difference between God and the marketers: The marketers want something from you, and God does not. Even more, the marketers want to tell you who you should be, and God wants to tell you who you are. When God says, "I am He who is," he means that he does not need you so that he might "become himself" or turn a profit or be satisfied. He just is. And what's more, each of us comes to exist because God is for us. *For us,* God is our life; *for us,* God is our security; *for us,* God is present.

Here's the thing that Catherine learned: When we enter into prayer with God, *God does not need us,* and *God does not need anything from us.* In other words, God is not using us for something. Instead, God comes to us even though we owe God everything. We are *not* and God is; and yet we *are* because God is *for us.*

Listen, then, to the next line of what Catherine hears God speak to her: "Have this knowledge in your soul and the Enemy will not be able to trick you." All the tricks of the Enemy — who wants only to deceive us and control us — play upon one and only one thing: that we forget that God is God, and we are not.

How easy it is to make up our own rules for life. How tempting it is to let some other person or some other force tell us who we are and how to be happy. How convenient it is to just go with the flow and see where we end up. These are all little ways of forgetting that God is God, and we exist and live only because God is *for us.*

The Heart of Prayer

Do you see why I have been making such a big deal out of not thinking of prayer as a relationship among equals? God is God, and we are God's creatures. God creates us. In Jesus Christ, God claims us as his own beloved children. And by the Holy Spirit, God breathes his life into us. The right way to enter into prayer is to enter as someone in need.

You may remember the parable of the Pharisee and the tax collector in Luke 18:9–14. Two men go to the temple to pray. The first man, a Pharisee, is very pleased with himself. In fact, the Gospel text says that he "prayed thus *with himself*," and then he goes on to recount all of his own virtues. He has come there to tell God that he, the Pharisee, is enough. More than enough, even. And he thanks God for not making him like other people who are less than him, people who steal and lie and sin ... people like the tax collector, who is also at the temple praying.

That second man — the tax collector — does not say much. All he says is "God, be merciful to me, a sinner." That's his whole prayer. He stands at a distance, his eyes are downcast, and he beats his breast. If he knows anything, he knows that he is not enough. In fact, he believes that he is *not*: not virtuous, not deserving, not entitled. But the other thing he knows at the same time is that while he is *not,* God *is.* When he approaches God, he approaches as a beggar. And Jesus says the tax collector went home justified, but not the Pharisee.

This, my friend, is the real point of what I have been trying to say about prayer. The point is that to learn how to pray, we have to learn how to approach God as beggars. We are in need, and God is the one who does not need anything from us. God is the one who desires only to give us all that we need. If we remember that, we can never be tricked. But to remember that, we cannot just think about it; we must also practice it. I mean, we must practice *begging God*.

That is the heart of prayer: begging God. We can enter into prayer when we stop trying to approach God as an equal, or treating God as someone who needs something from us. Instead, we ought to approach God as the one from whom we need everything. I know that sounds really unbecoming of mature and dignified people like us, but that's kind of the point. God is God, and we are his creatures.

This is a hard lesson. I know that. It is hard for me, too. I do not want to be a beggar; I want to be self-sufficient. One practice I started adopting is that every day I try to *beg* God for what I need — or at least what I think I need. I don't just pray about what I need — I actually beg. How do you beg? Part of begging is in your body: You kneel, you lie flat on the floor, you open your hands, you press your hands firmly together, you bow your head, you lower your eyes. In sum, you ask in all humility, even as you ask in confidence.

For you or me to pray — really pray — means approaching God *as* God and accepting ourselves as God's creatures: beloved, but nothing without him. Our relationship with God is on God's terms. Prayer begins by accepting those terms.

5

How to Pray — Part 2

What I wrote about prayer earlier had a bitter taste. That taste came from the instruction to become a beggar. Neither you nor I like to beg. It is humiliating, we become vulnerable, and it wounds our pride. We lose control when we beg, because we put ourselves at someone else's mercy. We would rather make a bargain, earn our share, or scheme our way to our desired end. We would like to approach God more on the level, as if God were not so very different from us, and our prayer could be more of a "relationship" like other relationships: with give and take, and a sense of mutuality. The instruction to become a beggar disrupts all that. What I wrote earlier brought the bitter taste of our belittlement in prayer.

I hope what I write to you now carries the sweetness of our belovedness in prayer.

Our belovedness is not found in anything we say about ourselves; instead, it comes through what we say to God. What is this thing we say to God? It comes right at the start of the most basic and simplest of all Christians prayers. We address God as "Our Father."

You have heard those words and likely said them countless times over the course of your life, as have I. Like me, you can probably rattle off the several dozen words that follow those first two words without a moment's thought, just like you were reciting the alphabet. It seems there is nothing new there; it is just the formulaic stuff of rote memorization. "Our Father" has become a filler — just a passing phrase.

I am not telling you anything you don't already know when I say that Jesus gives his disciples the prayer that begins with "Our Father." And maybe you also know that, at least in the Gospel of Luke, Jesus teaches this prayer after his disciples see him praying and one of them says to him, "Lord, teach us to pray" (Lk 11:1). But maybe you haven't much considered just how significant and revolutionary it is that Jesus forms his disciples to say "Our Father."

What matters here is who Jesus is. If he is just another enlightened religious teacher — even a magnificent figure — then teaching his disciples to call God "Father" is equivalent to him telling them to call God "Great One" or "Life-giver" or "Our Friend." It would add something to our imaginations and give us a useful way to think about God as we try to pray.

If, however, Jesus truly is the *Son* of God, then something remarkable is happening when he forms his disciples to call God "Our *Father.*" The Son of God is not like us, but became like us. He is not just another man, but the Word of God who became flesh. His Father is *not* "our" Father. God the Father is Jesus' Father. When Jesus addresses God as "Father," he is revealing what is eternally true: He is the only Son of the Father. God is our Creator, and we are God's creatures. It is actually not the "Father" part of Jesus' teaching on prayer that is so shocking. What is really shocking is that he says "*Our* Father."

Communion in Prayer

We would be right to think that the "Our" in that address means that we address the Father together — in other words, I cannot claim the Father as my own, excluding you. That is utterly significant for how we ought to think of, care for, and treat each other. But the "Our" is even more significant than that. When Jesus teaches his disciples to pray, he does not form them to pray *alone.* Rather, he forms them to pray *with* him; indeed, he forms them to pray *in* him. The disciples of Jesus are to pray in Jesus' place — that is, they are to pray not as they themselves are on their own, but as Jesus himself is. Jesus is the Son who teaches his disciples to call *his* Father *our* Father. He is praying with us, and we are praying with him. Disciples never pray alone.

You may suspect that I am drifting far away from the practical stuff here. I assure you: Nothing is more practical than this. When his disciples asked him to teach them how to pray, Jesus did not teach them a technique. He drew them into his relationship with the Father. To accept Jesus' invitation to prayer means that God is not remote, distant, unreachable. Jesus says to his disciples: "Draw near. I give you *my* Father." This changes everything about who we are — it is the most practical thing of all. Jesus *makes* us the beloved sons and daughters of *his* Father. That is what Christian prayer is: being drawn into Christ.

In Christ, we become the ones who can call God "Father." That does not mean we cease being beggars. Christ himself became a beggar. Though he was rich, he became poor (see 2 Cor 8:9) so he could beg like we have to beg. Our begging God is not so lowly or belittling as it first seemed, because the Son of God begs with us, as one of us.

On this earth, Jesus begged his Father in heaven for *everything*. He did not do anything on his own. In the desert, the devil tempted him to do it another way, but Christ refused: He only lived through what the Father gave him and willed (see Lk 4:1–13 and Mt 4:1–11). As he entered into the day of his death, he prayed, "Father, if you are willing, remove this chalice from me; nevertheless not my will, but yours, be done" (Lk 22:42). He begged, but most of all he trusted. His was always the begging of the beloved Son: He depended on his Father for everything, and he knew that his Father always heard him and loved him.

Jesus begged God, but even more he trusted God as his Father. This is the heart of Jesus' gift to his disciples when he teaches them to pray "Our Father." In everything and for everything, this is who they can trust. They can trust God as Father because Jesus has given his own trust to them. "Trust my Father," he says, "whom I give you as your Father."

So what does this mean for us, today? It means that when we pray, we are not praying to a capricious deity, or an impersonal force, or some far-off and vague being. If you and I accept Jesus' invitation to prayer, it means that we get to call *his* Father, *our* Father. That is who listens to our prayers: Jesus' Father, who loves us. We are his beloved.

What can you do to practice being God's beloved? Something very simple, actually. Practice praying only these two words: "Our Father." I mean it: Make that your entire prayer sometimes. Just pray "Our Father," and then rest in silence for a minute, five minutes, twenty minutes.

Don't overthink it, but just remember that when you say "Our," you are calling God "Father" with me and with everyone else who calls upon God. But the more significant thing is also taking place: You are calling God "Father" with Jesus. This is *his* Father, whom he gives us as our own.

When we pray "*Our* Father," we practice accepting Christ's gift, and we join him in prayer. That means, also, that he joins us in begging for what we need. It is an incredible deal: He gains nothing from us yet gives us everything that he has, while we gain everything and give him all our needs. In this prayer we receive the great gift Christ has to give us: his trust in his Father.

So if I close by telling you that "you are loved," do not take it as wispy and insubstantial sentiment. Take it as the expression of a great and almost unfathomable mystery. The Son of God shares his divine sonship with you. He makes you God's beloved. There is nothing bitter about that.

6

How to Pray — Part 3

Prayer is a full-contact encounter. Most of the time, if we pray, we offer some momentary thoughts, or the latest pressing emotion, or scattered words here and there. But prayer is no partial endeavor: God wants more from us. Actually, God wants more *for* us. God wants us to be fully, thoroughly, authentically ourselves in our prayer — to be fully, fully human. Through our prayer, God seeks to fully encounter us so that, in that encounter, we might discover what it means to be fully alive. That lesson requires full contact.

You have been patient through two chapters on prayer already. First, I emphasized the necessity of begging in prayer. Then, I pointed us to the mystery of Jesus giving us *his* Father as "*Our* Father." We have approached prayer as the gift and responsibility of begging and trusting a Father who loves us.

In this third and final chapter on prayer, we'll bring together what I have already written to you on prayer, and what we discussed in the chapters on how to listen and how to study and work. Prayer requires attention, but true attention requires everything we have: mind, heart, imagination, and body. I also want you to know that everything I recommend to you about prayer, I also do. None of this is my own innovation. Instead, these are all practices and habits I have been trying to acquire after learning from various saints how they prayed.

Praying for the Help to Pray

There are three specific petitions I always start with for my daily prayer. Together, they go something like this: "God my Father, I beg you to focus my mind, open my heart, and engage my imagination in this time of prayer, so that I might receive what you desire to give me."

I am keenly aware of how difficult it is to focus my mind. St. Teresa of Ávila was fond of telling her religious sisters whom she was teaching to pray that "our minds are so scattered, they are like wild horses no one can stop."[1] You know what that is like, don't you? You say to yourself, "Okay, I am going to focus on *this*," but almost immediately you find your thoughts racing in all directions. Teresa does not blame herself or her sisters for being easily distracted; in fact, she quite plainly tells them and us, "I consider distraction to be an incurable disease."[2]

We are distractable creatures — we just have to accept that. So one of the things I beg of the Lord at the beginning of my prayer is to help me focus my thoughts on him, whether that is through a portion of Scripture I am praying with, or a particular prayer from a saint or the Tradition I am reciting, or simply as I rest in his presence in a chapel or elsewhere in quiet. I cannot fully focus my mind by myself, so I always ask God to help me.

I find that I must also ask God to open my heart. I am stubborn and like to have things my way. Even when I am asking God to show me his will, I am very susceptible to only listening to what I want to hear. It is like I am filtering the word of God through my own predetermined desires, which usually prevent me from doing really difficult or self-sacrificial things that I would rather not do. That means that I am coming to God with a closed heart.

For my heart to really be open, I need to be ready to receive God on his own terms. If God is to show me what he wills for me, what is good for me, and what is good for others, then my part is to be ready to receive the good things he seeks to give me. Those good things are not always what I want. This is why in the "Our Father" we regularly pray: "Thy kingdom come, thy will be done … give us this day our daily bread." We can never stop working to place God's will before our own small and often selfish will, so that he can fill us with the bread that truly sustains us. I want too little, so I have to beg God to open my heart to more.

Of all things, though, I have found it hardest to make my imagination available to the Lord in prayer. I like to think about and analyze things. I enjoy coming to my own insights and feeling smart. I am not as comfortable yielding to images and scenes, or even colors and moods to shape and inspire my imagination. St. Ignatius of Loyola has helped me to see that I tend to keep my imagination out of prayer. I can go deep into an intense television drama (and I really only like superintense TV), and then I run those narratives and images in my imagination over and over again with ease. But when it comes to giving that same kind of access to the Lord who speaks to me in Scripture, in scenes of the Gospel, through the Rosary, or in the examination of my own conscience, I am not so ready with my imagination. I have had to beg and beg and beg for the Lord to take hold of my imagination. As it turns out, some of the most important and vivid periods of prayer I have enjoyed in the past few years have been the ones where the Lord engaged my imagination to encounter me. I have to keep begging for this grace, because it does not come easily to me. (And I've also had to stop getting so deep into intense TV dramas so that my imagination is free for the Lord when I seek to pray — I only have so much "bandwidth.")

For each of these modes of being available and attentive to the Lord in prayer — through my mind, in my heart, and with my imagination — I know that my body often leads the way. Rather than trying to rush through prayer, I try to slow my breathing. Rather than being tensed up and anxious, I try to open my palms and face them forward, often while standing. Rather than slumping and slouching, I try to sit upright and alert, or kneel in a comfortable but intentional posture. Sometimes I even lie down with my face to the floor, but this only works if I am not tired. In all of these postures, I try to allow my body to mimic and express what I beg the Lord to allow my mind, heart, and imagination to do: Be present, intentional, alert.

Three Practical Practices for Praying

Prayer is availability to God, who makes himself available to us. It is hard to make ourselves available. Most of us are more familiar with only being partially available while spreading ourselves rather thin, or splitting our attention among multiple people or things. We have to work to learn this habit of availability, and that habit is nurtured through intentional practices. None of these practices is overtly pious or obviously spiritual. In fact, these are all rather natural practices. But as I have said before, the spiritual builds on the natural, and so these very natural practices prepare us for the spiritual ripening that God desires for us. You may notice how similar these practices are to some of the practices I recommended earlier, whether for learning how to listen or how to study and work. All these things are related and are part of the development of our character toward the fullness of life.

First, prepare to pray. You need to set aside a dedicated space for prayer that is uncluttered and free of distractions. And right along with that, be sure to leave some time *before* your period of prayer to break away from whatever you were previously doing. We certainly can and should bring the stuff of life into our prayer, but we should not hurry and rush the way we typically do with the stuff of life when we start to pray. Just like most of us need some winding-down time before we go to bed, so we need some time to prepare our minds, hearts, and imaginations before we enter into prayer.

Second, use a timer for prayer. Our obsession with time distracts us from prayer. We always want to know what time it is or how much time we have left. Remove this distraction by simply setting a timer and leaving that timer across the room or space from where you are praying.

Third and finally, write or sketch something at the end of every period of prayer. I have a small journal, and for every period of prayer, I write no more than one page. I have found that this regular practice does two things: One, it allows me to express some of the fruit or frustration of my prayer, and two, it provides me with a record of my prayer to review later. I cannot tell you how many times I have had thoughts or feelings or insights come to me in prayer that were prepared weeks or months earlier. With the journal, I am then able to go back and review those earlier periods of prayer, and often learn more about myself and my God in the process.

Rest assured that God will be ready for full contact in your prayer. Your only and entire duty is to work on bringing your whole self to him.

7

How to Begin to Love Your Neighbor

People seem to hate one another a lot these days. It is not merely that people have differing opinions and thus disagree with one another. It is more that people are pitted against one another, hating the *person* on the other side, as though the sheer existence of that person or group is itself the problem. Their existence is repugnant. The response is to seek to eliminate "the other."

With increasing regularity, we see people demand that those they hate cease to be heard, seen, or treated as fully human. Yes, this happens on very public levels with rival political factions or ideological groups. But it also happens in smaller communities and within peer groups, even friend groups or families.

Here's the worst part: We are tempted to do the same thing when confronted with the *kind* of people we don't like. I recognize this tendency in myself. I begin by assuming the worst about their motives. I am frustrated and even vexed because their way of being or thinking feels like a threat to me and the way I am. I feel the seduction of creating "in groups" and "out groups," of rallying around a sense of "us" that is opposed to "them." The more my access to information grows and my digital contacts multiply, the more my potential for disdain and quick judgments increases accordingly. I find this all exhausting and depressing, even numbing. What about you?

A Simple, Profound Habit

It turns out that we are not the first people to swim in social dynamics like these. I recently came across something that gave me a new perspective as I was reading about the life and witness of the Italian saint Gianna Beretta Molla. In fact, it was something her husband, Pietro, said about his own life that made a lasting impression on me.

Gianna and Pietro lived through the rise of fascism in Europe during the first half of the twentieth century. During their formative years as teenagers and twenty-something young adults, it became increasingly common for people to group together into tribes against "less desirable" members of their society. Across their nation and in their own community, neighbors were becoming enemies. It was routine to learn to hate one another.

But Pietro, like Gianna, was part of a movement called Catholic Action. The basis of this movement was to form communities of people who gathered regularly to pray and get to know one another, as well as serve those who were suffering in their communities. In reflecting on his regular participation in this truly countercultural form of community during his formative years, Pietro said this:

> If I had to sum up the essence of my formation as a Catholic layman in one single concept, I would choose "respect for my neighbor." … Catholic Action taught me great respect for others, and this attitude has been invaluable for me in my life. In the decades I spent in factories with positions of great responsibility, precisely respect for my neighbor saved me in the Fascist years, during the war, and in the period of great strikes.[1]

I don't want you to miss the simplicity and power of what Pietro is saying. The simplicity is that all he did was regularly get together with others — in person! — getting to know them for who they were and then doing works of service with or for them. The power, however, is that this regular rhythm of his life saved him from becoming a hateful and prejudiced person when the dominant influences in his society were leading most people to become just like that.

From Pietro Molla I've learned that the first step in learning how to love your neighbor is taking the time to grow in respect for your neighbor. Pietro did not resort to seeing people as "types"; instead, he spent time with different people whom he came to know as real, complex, and unique persons. This is what saved Pietro from the propaganda of his age.

I think about Pietro when I think about the kind of world you and I live in today. We can sit alone in our rooms and, through a handheld device, encounter news of and messages from people all across the world. It seems like we are encountering people, but we're not. We are encountering appearances and summaries. We are encountering algorithms that treat each of us as a certain "kind" of information consumer in order to feed us presorted versions of the world. We hear the tidy phrases and labels for people and groups that have been forged through a social milieu that demands "us" vs. "them" binaries.

But here's the secret: What we are *not* encountering from the comfort of our own rooms are actual flesh-and-blood people. We know "about" groups of people we have never met and are not likely to ever meet, but do we really know the people living next to us, who live around and among us? Pietro Molla was saved from losing his own dignity because he spent his time with such people — real people, whom he spent time with, in actual places.

Moving Beyond the Shades of Gray

C. S. Lewis wrote a spectacular little book called *The Great Divorce*. In this book, he imagines a gray town where people are always able to get what they think they want. The people of this town start off living near one another, but right away disagreements arise among them over any number of things. At the first sign of diverging opinions, the residents of this town pick up their houses and spread out from one another. They keep spreading out from one another more and more as their individual preferences and ideas conflict. This movement happens all the time so that, forever and ever, people are just moving away from one another, becoming more and more isolated. They create their own tiny, private neighborhoods: neighborhoods without neighbors. Lewis calls this gray town "Hell."

Hell is getting what you think you want and only getting what you think you want. What the residents of the gray town do not experience is conversion. They do not change. They just become more and more caricatures of themselves, digging deeper into their own self-selected preferences and opinions.

Pietro Molla experienced lifelong conversion. Yes, he was converted through prayer and his participation in the sacraments and the life of the Church, but he was also and crucially converted through real contact with the people he lived around and among. He was converted by his neighbors. As he said, he learned to "respect" them. He grew to notice their distinctiveness, and he slowly learned to care for them as real people, rather than seeing them as obstacles to his own preferences and cravings. He could have just separated himself from those who were not like him — honestly, it would have been easier, especially since the major movements in his society were encouraging him to do just that. But Pietro did the more difficult thing, which was really about a whole bunch of very small decisions to go toward his neighbors rather than away from them. In going toward them, he moved away from his biases.

Not Hating Is Not Enough

I almost titled this chapter "How to Not Hate People," but mutual nonaggression is not enough. The aim is to love your neighbor. Here, I am trying to share with you how we get started toward that end. I will build on what I have written here in subsequent chapters, but for now let me leave you with three practices for how to *begin to* love your neighbor.

Once every day, take ten minutes to examine your own judgments and dispositions relative to other people. Interrogate yourself to see if you have entertained thoughts or feelings about other people or "types" of people that incline you to disparage or maybe even begin to hate them. Ask yourself what the source of this irritation may be. Try to be specific. The more specific, the better. Maybe keep a small journal to help track your thoughts and identify patterns.

Once every week, intentionally spend dedicated and intentional time with people whom you regularly see at work or school or in your neighborhood, but who are not your typical "in crowd." In other words, mix it up and break out of your comfortable realm of social relations (people otherwise known as "friends"). This does not need to be anything magnificent; it can simply be striking up a conversation, taking a coffee break in a different group, or eating lunch in a different area. (Warning: I just got very close to employing the clichéd high school cafeteria example.)

Then, once every month, spend at least an hour in a place where you would otherwise not spend your time. Change your scenery and intentionally engage with the people who are there. You might go to a different bar, which is a different *kind* of bar from what you are used to. You might go to a homeless shelter or soup kitchen to spend time talking with the people who are eating or staying there. You might go to a city council meeting to listen to what is being discussed and talk with the people who show up. Ask the people in this new place what they care about and listen to their stories. That last bit right there is precisely what we are going to pick up on in the next chapter, on how to *actually* love your neighbor.

Pushing back against the tendencies to too quickly judge others while instead learning to pay attention to what other people care about is how love of neighbor is born. We might think that love of neighbor begins with a sweet passion or a rush of inspiration. Typically, it does not. It begins instead with making the small, unspectacular choice to move toward rather than away from those who are not like you, or who start to irritate you, or who are in some way inconvenient to be around. How that develops into true love of neighbor is the topic of the next chapter.

8

How to Actually Love Your Neighbor

A lawyer once approached Jesus and asked him what he must do to inherit eternal life. Jesus told him to love God and love his neighbor. But then the lawyer asked, "And who is my neighbor?" So Jesus told him that parable you and I know all too well, where a traveler is mugged and left for dead in a ditch on the side of a road, only to have two religious figures pass by on the other side. It was then that a Samaritan — an outsider, despised by the Jewish people of Jesus' time — paid attention to the dying traveler, went down into the ditch, tended to the man's wounds, lifted him up, and took him to an inn where he could be cared for and recover. As Jesus finished the narrative, he asked the lawyer, "Which one of the three was neighbor to the injured traveler?" And the lawyer answered, "The one who showed him mercy." Not only was that the correct answer to Jesus' immediate question, it was also the answer to the lawyer's own question from earlier: to inherit eternal life, you must love your neighbor — that is inseparable from loving God (see Lk 10:25–37).

What made the good Samaritan "good"? Four things: First, he paid attention to the suffering of the person he encountered. Second, he went *toward* rather than *away from* the one who was suffering. Third, he went down into the ditch to share in the injured man's suffering. Fourth, he gave his *time* and his *resources* to meet the injured man's real needs. When Jesus tells the lawyer to "Go and do likewise," he is telling him to do these things.

In the last chapter, I talked about how to *begin* to love your neighbor. We begin by spending time with people, especially people who are not in our typical "in crowd." We learn to see these "others" as real, distinctive, complex persons. Otherwise, we often end up thinking about people as "types" — this type of person, or that type of person. As we heard from Pietro Molla, just learning to "respect our neighbors" (as he called it) can save us from the most terrible kinds of prejudice, cruelty, and hatred. Pietro helped us see how to *begin* to love our neighbor.

In the parable of the good Samaritan, Jesus reveals to us what *actually* loving our neighbors demands. Actually loving is often time-consuming, costly, inconvenient, and unglamorous. It is also what our own eternal happiness depends on. If we do not learn to love our neighbors, we will never be happy.

The Deepest Question

The brilliant twentieth-century essayist and mystic Simone Weil had a devastatingly direct insight into the demands of the love of neighbor. She said that love of neighbor comes down to one question: "What are you going through?"

What she means is that for me to love someone as my neighbor, I need to pay close, close attention to what is actually going on with the other person. I cannot stop with what I *think* is going on with the person; I cannot interpret them too quickly. It is often easier to do the good I *want* to do than it is to do the good that someone else *needs*. Why? Because I prefer doing what I like to do; I like to set the terms, even when I am doing good. That is not love of neighbor.

Love of neighbor requires being present to and learning about what is actually good for the other person. You love another person by responding to what the other person needs and what would be good for him, not what you think he needs or just what you want to give him. This demands an almost unbelievable discipline: to really, truly pay attention to another person, and then act on that person's good.

Think about the good Samaritan. He noticed that the traveler was injured. While it seems obvious, we should note that for the Samaritan to see the injured traveler at all, the Samaritan had to be in the same place — on the same road — where the injured man was himself. It is really rather easy to avoid places where people suffer: Don't go downtown. Don't go to your dormmate's room when you hear her sobbing. Don't go to the living room when your dad looks stressed. Don't go near the loneliest person you know. The Samaritan, however, was in the place where suffering existed.

Being there was not enough, though. After all, the priest and the Levite were there as well, but they "passed by on the other side." When the Samaritan saw the injured man, however, he moved closer. He paid attention to the man's wounds. He got his hands dirty. The Samaritan got into the ditch with the injured man. Suddenly, the injured man was no longer in his misery alone — the Samaritan was there with him. The Samaritan was paying attention to what the man was going through.

After the Samaritan saw and learned about the traveler's wounds by being close up and paying attention, he then started to act. He bandaged the wounds. He lifted the injured man out of the ditch. He took him to where he could receive better help. He paid for the man's care. He pledged to do more if more was required. The Samaritan was committed to this stranger's well-being. That's what turned these strangers into neighbors.

The First Samaritan

You know who was the first good Samaritan? Jesus. I mean that, but not in some lame, sappy, overly pious way. Jesus himself is the outsider who is "not from around here." He was safe and sound, perfectly at peace and filled with joy by his Father's side in heaven. By his own will, this Son of God came to where we are and joined us in what we are going through.

The Son of God got into the ditch with us. He paid attention to our wounds — the wounds of sin and shame and sorrow. He got his hands dirty. He did not leave us in the ditch but lifted us out of it. He himself takes us to his Father's household, where we will be made fully well and learn to be happy. He is committed to us who were strangers to him. He loved us concretely, and that made us his neighbors.[1]

I learned something new about this several years ago when the then-provost of my university was addressing the incoming freshman class. Dr. Tom Burish looked out on a couple thousand nervous and excited 18- and 19-year-olds and told them that each of them, at some point or another, would suffer and struggle mightily during their years in college. He told them that it will seem at those times like you are alone, that no one is there for you and no one will understand. But he told them to look behind them to their parents and guardians and families who were there with them that day. He said, "You might think that your parents do a great many things for you because they love you, and that is true. But what you may not have considered is that your parents love you because they have done a great many things for you."

We might think that love of neighbor begins with the feelings of affection, so that the good acts done for the good of others are expressions or fruits of those affections. But Dr. Burish opened up a deeper insight: We learn to love people by doing acts of love for them. When we care for others, we take an interest in them — we invest in them. Those incoming freshmen heard two things that day: First, when you struggle, let others help you, because you will actually help them learn to love you; and second, care for one another, especially those whom you see struggling, because that is how you will learn to love them.

Does Jesus act for our good because he loves us, or does he love us because he has acted for our good? That question does not have an answer. He loves because he acts; he acts because he loves. What Jesus told that lawyer who was looking for eternal life is that if you want to be happy, love your neighbor. If you do not begin with love for your neighbor, act for your neighbor's good, and you will learn to love him or her. Learning to love your neighbor really matters because eternal life is for neighbors.

How do you "make" neighbors? Pay attention. Go toward suffering. Share the burdens with the ones who suffer. Be generous with your time and other resources; give all you can for the other person's well-being.

And at the same time, allow others to claim you as their neighbor. Let them see how you are suffering. Let them come close to you. Let them share your burdens. Receive the generosity of their time and resources.

In the real world we cannot always determine whether or not another person suffers, but we can *always* determine whether or not another person suffers alone. Love of neighbor is about sharing the burden. It is about sharing with others what they are going through, and letting others share in what you are going through.

9

How to Date

I want to talk with you about dating. Maybe you are already married, or for some other reason you are not interested in dating, but you still might find interest in what I write about here for the sake of supporting friends or thinking about how to raise children who will someday "date well." Regardless of your level of personal interest in this topic, I want to start by admitting an obvious but often neglected fact: Dating does not just happen when you want it to. Most people at some time or another *want* to date someone — whether a specific "someone" or not — yet they cannot just make it happen. After all, we are not talking about becoming a pet owner, because you really could get a pet pretty much any time you wanted to. By talking about dating, we are talking about developing a relationship with another human being who, unlike the pet, must be a willing and interested party. There is no store for "people whom you could date" next to the pet store in the mall. Even if there are apps or other means for matching with another person you might consider dating, none of these means comes with guarantees. Patience is always a hard virtue to cultivate but perhaps hardest of all when it comes to the desire to date. Yet patience can foster tenderness and new kinds of openness, which actually form you into an even more loving and compassionate person. Patience itself is preparation for dating, as it is a preparation for marriage and the religious life.

Tenderness and openness are not merely "soft" characteristics. These are forms of strength: the ability to welcome others into your life and to receive them as they really are. It is also about the ability to allow others to know and receive you as you are. And realizing the fruits of patience as tenderness and openness (among other things) helps us consider what dating is, and what it is not. It is *not* about you getting something. Rather, it is about you freely sharing in something that someone else is also freely sharing in. What you are sharing in together is learning about, enjoying, and willing the good for each other. That's my non-catchy definition of dating: a reciprocal relationship of learning about, enjoying, and willing the good for someone else. (I would never cut it as a producer of *The Bachelor*, by the way.)

Personally, I used to put *a lot* of pressure on every dating relationship I was ever in, beginning as early as short-lived crushes in middle school. Somewhere lurking in my mind was the expectation that for this to be a successful relationship, it had to be more and more intense, and then last forever. Any relationship that didn't last forever was a failure. Any relationship that didn't get more intense wasn't progressing. With deep-seated assumptions like that, you aren't really dating another person; you are dating a set of expectations and secretly subjecting the other person to those criteria.

Four Important Things about Dating, Then Another Thing

Holding things in secret is where the downfall of relationships begins. I think it is fair to say, therefore, that the first important thing when it comes to learning how to date is committing to telling the truth. This is not the same as brute honesty, where you feel compelled to tell the other person every single thing you are thinking or feeling all the time, including whether you think their laugh can be annoying or that they really don't look great in their favorite top. Telling the truth is about keeping things transparent. Respect the other person enough to let them be at peace around you, never giving them a reason to suspect that you are anything less than sincere. And respect yourself enough to mean what you say and say what you mean, rather than merely presenting yourself in one way when in fact that is not who you are or what you're about.

Telling the truth is as much about being forthcoming about your motivations and intentions as anything else. That means that in order to be honest, you have to avoid constructing little hidden agendas and telling little white lies. Deception sneaks in to relationships stealthily and corrodes them from the core. A commitment to truth-telling is absolutely fundamental to a healthy dating relationship (as with any relationship), and so too, therefore, is the humility and courage to ask for forgiveness when you have not been completely honest, and to bestow forgiveness when the other person falls short in that regard, too. The exchange of forgiveness is a form of truth-telling.

The second important thing in learning how to date is to follow through. There are at least two parts to following through. On the one hand, in order to be a person who regularly follows through, you need to be careful about what you promise. Consider what it takes to fulfill the promise you are making, and consider what it will cost you to see that promise all the way through, come what may. Promising fewer things but fulfilling more of your promises is a sign of maturity, responsibility, and respect.

On the other hand, to be a person who follows through you need to, well, actually follow through. Only rarely does follow-through come without obstacles. If you make plans for the weekend with the person you are dating, it is probably the case that early on in the relationship, you couldn't imagine ever wanting to do anything else. But later in the relationship, the excitement will have settled, which makes you less psyched about following through on your word when you hear later about what your other friends are planning for the weekend. Suddenly, you don't want to follow through on your original plans. And here comes a prime occasion for beginning to shy away from transparency. You want to make a little excuse about why you *can't* do what you said you would do that weekend. What you are not saying is that you actually just *want* to do something else more. Now, to follow through on what you promised, you would need to sacrifice what you suddenly want to do more in order to honor the plans you made. Or, if necessary and prudent, you should actually talk to (don't text) your significant other and tell them the real reason you want to change your plans. Be honest. Being up front and having a dialogue is itself a way of following through. This is the harder path, but it is more responsible, and it strengthens trust.

The third important thing in learning how to date is that when you are with the other person, be with them. You might think back to what I wrote to you about how to listen and how to work and study. I pointed out that most of us are so used to splitting our attention among any number of things that we really struggle to be attentive to where we are, what we are doing, and the person (or people) we are with at any given time. We want to check what's going on elsewhere, and we want to keep soft contact with lots of different folks. What this means, in the end, is that we become people who are never really present. The fact of the matter is that you cannot learn about, enjoy, and will the good of another person if you are not present to them. In other words, you aren't really dating someone if, when you're with them, you habitually split your attention.

A key to dating is practicing really being *there*. Believe me, I do not mean becoming the kind of people who, when they are together, cease to recognize the existence of other human beings or the cosmos in general. Those people are annoying and, in fact, unhealthy. What I do mean is that you have to regularly say "no" to distractions or competing demands in order to say "yes" to truly being with the other person.

A fourth important thing in learning how to date is to pray for the other person. Bear with me: I am not intending to be lame or unduly pious. I am talking about relocating your own center of concern through prayer. For most of us most of the time, the center of our concern is ourselves. You have to counter that engrained tendency by sometimes even *forcing yourself* to pay attention to the other person's needs and desires. Pay attention when you are together, and reflect on them and what is good for them when you are apart. Then pray for them: for *their* good, not only for your own good that happens to overlap with theirs. In fact, *beg* God on their behalf. Praying for the other person like this is the most significant way in which you can will their good. The second most significant way to will their good is, after you pray for them, doing whatever you can do to serve them, help them, or support them in whatever way they need.

The last thing I will mention as important for learning how to date is to do ordinary things together, even early on. Dating does not always have to be about doing big things together, with everything feeling like "a date." In fact, too much of that "big date" feel contributes to false expectations and, honestly, a lot of play-acting. While it is not wise to suggest that your first date be a trip to the bureau of motor vehicles to renew your driver's license (this will only succeed in showing the other person right away that you are a person without any sense for human interactions), it is not at all a bad idea to do mundane things like that (or maybe things slightly less soul-sucking) as early as the first few weeks of a relationship. Do things where you don't have to dress up, you don't have to be on your best behavior, and you don't have other people waiting on you. This is a way to start to "be real" with each other earlier, so there isn't some sharp break between the early-relationship-magical-fantasy and the real life into which things eventually settle anyway. Practice being normal, early and often.

I haven't talked much about romance here. You probably don't want to hear that from me anyway. What I have tried to talk about is how to allow dating to enrich and develop your character (tell the truth, follow through, pay attention, etc.). Even wanting to date and waiting to meet someone is a time to develop patience, to cultivate tenderness and openness. At some point for some people, there will be a call and then a decision to commit yourself to the other person you have been dating for life through marriage. Should that call and commitment come, you may then continue what you have already started: becoming people of character and generosity, together, for the good of others. For the majority of relationships that do not move toward marriage, healthy dating relationships — though *never* perfect — will form both people in becoming better at learning about, enjoying, and willing the good of another person.

So here's the truly last thing that is really, perhaps, the first thing. To date other people, you have to take a risk. You have to *ask* someone else on a date. You have to say *yes* when someone else asks you. One date may be one date. That's fine. Try again and be open. But there is no way to start learning how to date without actually being willing to date. There is always a risk involved because relationships — even short-lived ones — have to do with other real human beings who are never just what we expect or exactly what we think we want. Developing relationships with other real people requires us to change and to grow. Thank God.

10

How to Have Sex

If you picked up this book because you saw this chapter, the title may have deceived you. You will not find any diagrams here, nor will you discover descriptions of techniques. For things like that, you'll have to look elsewhere, but before you do, I would encourage you to examine your motives.

I am not writing to tell you how you can have toe-curling sex or anything like that. Catholic and other Christian writers who promise such things are deceiving you, even if they don't mean to. They are deceiving you in the way of desire by leading you to desire the wrong thing in the wrong way. Catholics do not merely have alternative means for seeking out the same end in sex as popular culture, as if this was all really about max-imizing pleasure.

At the same time, though, the Catholic understand-ing of sex is not *not* about pleasure. Rather, this is all about fulfillment, which is not opposed to pleasure but goes beyond it. This is also about joy, which is not op-posed to happiness but goes beyond it. Fulfillment and joy require sacrifice, but that is not the same as nev-er-ending self-denial, whereby life becomes drudgery. This is about the fullness of life.

With those preliminaries out of the way, I want to give you a twofold guide on how to have sex. First, be there. Second, pledge yourself. Now let me explain what I mean.

Be There

You might think it obvious that if you are to have sex, you are going to "be there." Leaving aside the strange ways in which people are "there" or "not there" for sex in the digital age, don't we have a sense of what it means to be somewhere but not actually *be there*? To really "be there" requires both attentiveness and transparency.

Attentiveness has to do with the singular focus of your entire self: mind, body, spirit. Transparency means being free of deception or duplicity — being complete-ly honest with and available to another person. Atten-tiveness and transparency are the twin disciplines for intimacy.

It is common for modern Christian writers to talk

about something like intimacy when talking about the true meaning of sex. They typically point to the closing verse of the second creation account in Genesis to support their claim (that's the account that leads to Adam and Eve). That's where we're told that the man and his wife were *naked without shame* (see Gn 2:25). What this means seems obvious: They could bare their bodies to each other without bashfulness or lust. The quick move then is for popular writers and speakers to say something like "this is what sex within marriage gives you: sex without sin or guilt."

I got that message a lot growing up, first from the nondenominational youth group I attended with my friends in middle school, and later throughout college from popular Catholic chastity speakers. What silently formed in my mind was a vague notion that getting married was like gaining admission to an amusement park: Once you're in, you can seek after pleasure without impediments or regret.

But here is the crucial thing that is almost always left out of the "naked without shame" mantra. When at the close of Genesis 2 we encounter the word *naked* in English, what is being translated is the Hebrew word *arummim*. When we then move to the first verse of Genesis 3, where the serpent is introduced, and we read that it was "the shrewdest of all the wild beasts," the word we read as the superlative form of *shrewd* is the Hebrew word *arum*. What we miss in English is that to be "naked" [*arummim*] in this context means to be without guile or shrewdness [*arum*].

What does it mean to be shrewd or full of guile? It means to be hiding something: namely, to be hiding what you're really about. Your words or your actions say one thing, but your heart and your intentions say something else. If we investigated the question the serpent asks at the beginning of Genesis 3 and then his further arguments, that is precisely what we see: The serpent is deceiving about its enterprise.

So what does it mean to be naked without shame? Yes, absolutely, it means for the man and the woman to bare their bodies to one another, but it also and crucially means that they *know* each other. They are transparent to each other, and they are attentive to each other. They are not hiding anything. What they say and how they act, what they think and what they intend are all aligned. They are "there" in every sense of the word.

Intimacy like this is far more than merely gaining admission to an amusement park. Rather, this is about becoming the kind of people capable of complete attentiveness and full transparency. Sex is about this kind of union: the full intimacy of being there.

Pledge Yourself

In a book about her conversion, my friend Abigail Favale wrote candidly about the sexual misadventures of her early young adult years. In particular, she talked about the lie and confusion of contraceptive sex, which is intentionally closed off from conceiving new life.

Abigail says that at that point in her life, rather than understanding and appreciating her own body and how it worked, the only thing that mattered to her was swallowing a pill to make sure that her body malfunctioned. While talking about one particular relationship that is representative of several others, Abigail wrote this:

> There's a language that the body speaks during sexual union. A wordless promise of total self-gift. The body says: I am wholly yours; I belong to you; I give myself, even my capacity to create new life, a gift that can't be taken back. When there are no spoken promises alongside this corporeal speech, the language of the body becomes a lie. With his body, he said: I give myself to you. With his words, he said: I don't want you.[1]

Abigail is describing sex without the pledge of yourself. In particular, what the man she was with was doing looked like full acceptance of Abigail, but at the very same time he was rejecting her in her fullness. He did not want her capacity to bear life within her body; he did not want her beyond this moment; he did not want to pledge himself to her, come what may. And, as Abigail attests, she did not want to pledge herself in that way either: to new life, to continued commitment, to the future.

The severing of sex from the possibility of conceiving new life is the great lie of the last one hundred years.

I know I might sound like a cranky, prudish religious complainer when I say that, but I want to tell you the truth. The truth is that sex closed off to new life diminishes our dignity. It is the mission of every generation to give rise to another generation. That mission means bringing about the next generation's existence *and* endowing that generation with what is most grand and beautiful. Every generation must give life and teach the next generation the way of life.

The sexual union between man and woman is the genesis of an entire society. Two persons, equal in dignity though distinct in identity, cooperate to bring new life into existence. But the crucial next dimension is that the responsibility to that new life continues, because what begins in the sexual union is completed in the commitment to give the child what is best and form him or her for the fullness of life.[2]

Sex necessarily entails a pledge of yourself, if sex is to be true. You pledge yourself to being there for the other person in all his or her fullness, and you pledge yourself with the other person to be there for the good of the new life that may come to be. This is how we become "like God," who creates life and nurtures his creatures to the fullness of life.

Disclosure

You may have noticed that I ended up presenting the unitive and procreative dimensions of sex, which accords with Catholic teaching. Moreover, the only condition in which you can fully "be there" with and for the other person and "pledge yourself" to the other person and with the other person for the next generation is within a committed, stable, and permanent relationship — namely, marriage. Have I therefore just tried to sneak in what you might already consider a stale and outdated teaching about sex? That was not my intention.

My intention is to tell you the truth and be truthful. I wanted to give an account of what sex is and how you have sex, in its fullness. It is about a union that is in the flesh but more than flesh, and it is about a pledge that happens now but does not end now. Anything less is too little.

There is clearly much more that could be said about all of this, and I am fully aware that significant and deeply personal issues abound in this discussion. There are many more paragraphs that cannot fit in this chapter or even this book, including ones you yourself might write. For now, then, I hope you will receive my words in the same spirit of generosity with which I have sought to give them, and by all means feel free to contact me to discuss more.[3]

11

How to Be Eucharistic — Part 1

The most addictive app on my phone is not tied to social media or news or sports or games. The most addictive app on my phone is Amazon. That app has formed my habits more than any other. It allows me to move from impulse to purchase in under ten seconds. A thought occurs to me, a "need" presents itself to me, convenience nudges at me, and the Amazon app lets me react immediately and then do nothing else. I want, I click, I effortlessly receive.

I am not addicted to any one of the objects I find on Amazon; instead, it's the ease I'm hooked on. It's all so easy. It takes away friction in my life. I don't have to long or wait or hope — I just click and I'm satisfied. This is the promise of technology: to make everything easy everywhere.

To be Eucharistic, you and I must resist the allure of ease. Christ has no interest in making us into mere consumers; he means instead for us to become capable of loving him. Love knows nothing of ease.

In the previous two chapters, I talked with you about how to date and how to have sex. In both chapters, I stressed the importance of attentiveness and follow-through. The beauty of dating and, to a greater degree, conjugal union is tied up with how we must grow in virtue, becoming more responsible and more real.

The same holds true with becoming Eucharistic: This is the path of becoming more yourself, more alive, more engaged, more responsible. The difference here, of course, is that the Eucharistic encounter is, first of all, the encounter with the Lord himself. He is the source and summit of everything, and this encounter is the most foundational of all. Even still, I will continue to speak of the importance of attentiveness and follow-through — or as I call it here: preparation and translation.

That is how we become Eucharistic: We prepare and we translate. In this chapter, I will talk about preparation, and in the next one, I will talk about translation.

Preparing a Dwelling Place

We probably all know at least a little bit about the Book of Exodus. The Israelites are enslaved in Egypt, the Lord calls Moses, the Israelites are led out of Egypt, and then they are definitively separated from their enslavers when they pass through the Red Sea. We might be surprised to learn that these events don't even bring us halfway through the book; the crossing of the Red Sea happens in chapter 14, but Exodus has forty chapters. Most of the narrative occurs after the Israelites have been freed from Egypt.

Now, you may easily guess that in the remaining twenty-six chapters, there is something about the Ten Commandments and a golden calf. But even those are part of a larger issue: the issue of freedom. Yes, the Israelites were freed from slavery in Egypt, but that raises the question: What were they freed for?

Back when Israel was in Egypt, the Lord God already proclaimed what he was freeing his people for: "I will ... deliver you ... and I will take you to be my people, and I will be your God" (Ex 6:6–7; and cf. 19:4–6, JPS). The ultimate reason for the Israelites' freedom is so that they might become God's chosen people. But God will not take them by force. He will not enslave them. To become God's chosen ones, they must freely accept the Lord as their God.

The Israelites must choose the Lord as their God by welcoming him into their midst. This is meant quite seriously and unambiguously: The Israelites are to construct a dwelling place — or tabernacle — so that the Lord God may come and be with them. Therefore, the Lord says to Moses: "Speak to the sons of Israel, that they take for me an offering; from every man whose heart makes him willing you shall receive the offering for me. ... And let them make me a sanctuary, that I may dwell in their midst" (Ex 25:2, 8).

Notice what the Lord says to Moses: The materials for this sanctuary can only come from those whose hearts make them willing. God wants to come to them, but they must be willing to receive and welcome him. And to do that, they have to prepare a place for him, from their hearts.

When the Israelites created a golden calf to worship, they did so with the materials God asked them to use to create a place for him. They were tired of waiting for God, so they made something else that they wanted to worship instead of the Lord who saved them. They made something in their own image, by their own designs, rather than waiting for the Lord's designs to be given to them. They chose ease in getting what they wanted right away, rather than preparing and waiting for the Lord.

Even still, God's desire to dwell among the people persisted, and the invitation to prepare to receive him remained. That is in fact what occurs in the final chapters of Exodus. The people make offerings to the Lord from their generous hearts, the people labor strenuously and skillfully to construct a dwelling place for

God, and the Lord comes to dwell in the midst of the people.

The Coming of Jesus Christ

What began in Exodus is completed in Jesus Christ: God comes to dwell with his people. But what was true in Exodus is also true of Christ: We must prepare to receive him. He will not take us by force, he will not enslave us, and so we must choose to receive the Lord as our God by welcoming him.

This is why being Eucharistic requires preparation. To accept the Lord as our God means that we must open our hearts to him. He seeks us, but we must be willing to receive him. Preparation was not easy for the Israelites in Exodus, and it is not easy for us. It is not a matter of click and done, as it is with my Amazon app. Rather, it is a matter of careful craftsmanship, generous giving, and patient waiting.

So how do we prepare for the Lord in the Eucharist? Maybe there's no better starting point than to follow the prayer of St. Thérèse of Lisieux, who prayed and prepared regularly to receive the Eucharist in this way:

> When I am preparing for holy Communion, I picture my soul as a piece of land and I beg the Blessed Virgin to remove from it any rubbish that would prevent it from being free; then I ask her to set up a huge tent worthy of heaven, adorning it with her own jewelry; finally, I in-

vite all the angels and saints to come and con-
duct a magnificent concert there. It seems to
me that when Jesus descends into my heart he
is content to find himself so well received and I,
too, am content.[1]

Thérèse prepares as diligently as the Israelites did in the
desert. As they prepared land to construct God's dwelling place, so she considers her soul that very land, and
she desires to remove the rubbish — the sins — from
her soul through confession. As the Israelites construct-
ed a dwelling place with their treasures, so Thérèse begs
Mary to bring her the grace to construct a dwelling
place for the Lord in her own soul, just as Mary made
her own body and soul into God's dwelling place. And
just as all the Israelites' artists and artisans beautified the
Lord's dwelling place, so Thérèse asks those great artists
of the faith — the saints, along with the angels — to help
her soul to shine and sing for the Lord.

This might sound rather pious, even overly sweet.
But think again about what Thérèse is saying and doing.
She is taking the time, putting in the effort, and beginning to ask for help to prepare a place fit for the Lord
God to come dwell. That "place" is her own body and
soul. That is where Jesus Christ wants to dwell: in her,
and likewise in us.

Receiving holy Communion is nothing like grab-
bing something off the shelf in a store or clicking "buy
now" through an app. Instead, it is a heart-to-heart en-

counter. With his whole heart, our Lord and our God seeks to dwell with us, and with our whole heart, we welcome him.

Becoming Eucharistic is not merely about receiving the Eucharist; it is also about preparing to receive our Eucharistic Lord. Taking the time to pray before receiving him matters. Going to confession to clear out the "rubbish" matters. Asking Mary to show us the grace to receive her Son, perhaps through praying the Rosary, matters. And asking for the intercession and guidance of the angels and the saints to love Christ as they love him — that matters, too.

Amazon has hooked me on ease, but the Lord wants me to prepare to meet him with my whole self. You and I slowly become Eucharistic by preparing well to receive the Eucharist.

12

How to Be Eucharistic — Part 2

D o you want to really live?

If you were to ask me that question, I would instinctively respond, "Yes, of course I want to really live." But if I examine my heart and mind, I am not sure that is actually true. Much of the time what I really want is to be comfortable, rewarded, approved of, or untroubled. Do I want to *really* live? Much of the time I actually just want to get by.

In the actual world where being truly present to someone for a genuine encounter requires the work of preparation and discipline on our part, we shrink from wanting to really live. We settle for something easier. The first part of being Eucharistic was about pushing back against that tendency and learning to prepare well to receive the Lord in the Eucharist. We become Eucharistic by preparing well to encounter the Lord.

Likewise, in the actual world, when really living requires commitment, a change of priorities, acting for the well-being of others, or getting our hands dirty in any number of ways, our desire to really live quickly dulls. Follow-through is hard, and it is costly. The second part of how to be Eucharistic, then, is about letting what — *who* — we receive in the Eucharist actually change us. Saint Augustine described this as "becoming what you receive," but here I will talk about it as "translation." We translate the life we receive into our own life.

Learning to Dance

During a retreat I once took, I spent some time talking with a Trappist monk, Fr. Matthew Kelty. He had been a worldly man, a man of letters, and a man steeped in New England culture prior to entering the monastery. So I asked him, "What was it like for *you* to enter the monastery?"

Father Matthew responded, "Well, the first thing is you just have to learn how to do everything. You have to learn how and when to eat, how and when to sleep, how and when to pray, how and when to work. There are all these steps in monastic life that you just don't know, and it takes a whole year before you feel like you are starting to get it all."

He stopped speaking, and a bit of silence followed. Eventually I said, "So then what? What happens after a year?" His eyes sparkled with mirth as he responded, "Well, baby, then it's time to dance."

When this very worldly man who had all these very strong and well-rehearsed habits entered the monastery, he was not at all accustomed to the ways of this new place. He was used to eating and speaking and acting in a different way — that other way was comfortable to him. When he entered into this new environment, he had to learn and learn and learn. It was not an easy fit, especially not at first. But what was the point of it all? As Father Matthew said, the point was to make this way of life his own. *He* had to dance.

St. Benedict of Nursia — one of the founders of monasticism in the West — talked about just this sort of thing in the beginning of his Rule for those who enter this Christian way of life. He begins by writing, "Listen carefully to the master's instructions, and attend to them with the ear of your heart."[1] It is the master — the Lord — who speaks first, and our primary duty is to listen and receive him. Soon thereafter, Benedict writes what this deep listening and receiving is really all about: "The Lord waits for us daily to translate into action, as we should, his holy teachings."[2]

Father Matthew took on new rhythms and habits, and he called it "dancing," while Saint Benedict talks about hearing the Lord and translating his words into action. What does this have to do with the Eucharist? The Eucharist is the gift and the way of giving that we only fully receive when we allow this gift and giving to change us.

The Lord Who Gives

What does Christ give in the Eucharist? The simple answer: everything. He holds nothing back. To his apostles gathered in the Upper Room, and to everyone who comes to receive from the altar today, he says, "This is my Body ... this is my Blood ... given for you."

This is no mere gesture. He backs up what he says by doing it. He gives his Body upon the cross; he gives his Blood for us. In his own words, Jesus explains the meaning of his death. His death is an offering. Whose offering? It is the Father's offering, his Father in heaven who gave his only Son for the life of the world. Jesus knew this, for as he told Nicodemus, "God so loved the world that he gave his only-begotten Son" (Jn 3:16). The Body and Blood of Jesus are the Father's pledge and gift of love for the sake of a world. The Father gives everything.

This offering is not the Father's only; this is also fully Jesus' offering: "I lay [my life] down of my own accord" (Jn 10:18). He gives his Body and his Blood — "given for you," he tells his disciples. Between the Father and the Son, there is a communion of giving.

Rather than participate in this communion of giving, others took Jesus by force. Jesus' Body and Blood are God's offer of love at the very same time that the world takes and does what it wants with that Body; the world sheds that Blood for its own purposes. Think about how peculiar this all is: Just when the Father and Son make this complete offer of love for the world, the world rejects Jesus. The love of God meets the world's lack of love in the Body and Blood of Jesus Christ.

The crucifixion of Jesus is the culmination of a history of sin. This is the remarkable thing: Precisely *then* — in the very same event — God makes the complete offer of love. By the witness of the apostles, in the testimony of the Gospels, in the preaching of the Church, in the Christian Tradition: The news of who the crucified one is breaks forth. The one we in this world killed is the Son of God given for us.

To each and every one of us, this much may be said: You took his Body, *but he gave it to you.* You shed his Blood, *but he shed it for you.* Receive him for who he is, and his death will bring you new life.

Jesus is the gift of love, and he is given totally and unreservedly to undeserving people. He is a pure gift, and he is all in. By the gift of himself in the Eucharist, the Lord says directly to each of us: This is the way to really live. I give you myself. Receive me, then go and do likewise. Give yourself.

"The true purpose of the Mass," a Jesuit priest once explained, "is not to make Christ offer himself anew for us: He has offered himself 'once for all' (Heb 10:10); nor is it to make us offer Christ instead of ourselves, but to make us offer ourselves with him and through him."[3]

The point is to become what we receive, to dance, to translate this love into the offering of ourselves in love. That is how we *receive* rather than *break from* communion: We learn to give ourselves.

The Whole Eucharist

For those of us who receive Christ in the Blessed Sacrament, we receive everything he gives us. That means that we receive not *something* but *someone*. To receive that gift, we must allow ourselves to become for others what he is for us. What we do for others, and the way we serve others, must say, "I am for you."

Pope Benedict XVI explained this communion between the Lord's gift of himself to us and our gift of ourselves for others when he wrote: "A Eucharist which does not pass over into the concrete practice of love is intrinsically fragmented."[4] In other words, if we receive him in the Eucharist but do not love our neighbor through concrete practices, we break the communion we receive. Without concretely acting in love toward others, we have received Christ's gift but not his way of giving. We have not allowed the Lord to become the source of our life. We only *really* live when we welcome Christ fully and then translate his love in ourselves through our love for others.

How does this translation take place? Through the works of mercy. We become Christ's love when we feed the hungry, give drink to the thirsty, give alms to the poor, shelter the homeless, visit the sick, visit the imprisoned, and bury the dead. We become Christ's love when we instruct the ignorant, counsel the doubtful, admonish the sinner, forgive trespasses, comfort the sorrowful, bear wrongs patiently, and pray for the living and the dead. These works of mercy are concrete practices of love, they are all costly, and they are all lifegiving. These are the ways of joining in Christ's offering of himself to us. This is how we dance.

At least once each week, we should each concretely perform at least one work of mercy. We should practice different works of mercy from week to week, rather than settling into the one we like best or that somehow "suits us." It is wise and prudent to put a work of mercy on the calendar for each week — in other words, to plan in advance to prioritize a work of mercy and commit yourself to following through in performing that work. Not only do these works stretch us, but they also allow us to say "thank you" to the Lord for his gift and way of giving for us. We thank him through our love for others. That, after all, is what "Eucharist" means: thanksgiving.

13

How to Read Scripture

I teach a course on theology and art. Some of my students are hesitant to analyze art, thinking that their insights will be superficial or unsophisticated. Others are a little too eager to interpret; they assume every interpretation is equally legitimate. No matter where the students begin, they must each learn to start with what they see.

Starting with what they see is not simple. The first assignment teaches them that. They spend three hours looking at one seemingly uncomplicated piece of art. I call this assignment the "Intense Look," and the whole point is just to *see* the painting you have selected. Students keep a journal of their viewing periods, tracking what they notice and when.

Students typically begin with a bit of fear, then move to boredom, then more boredom, but eventually strange things start happening. They begin noticing symmetries in the painting they hadn't seen before, like a piece of fruit being the exact same shape as a gown's ruffle. They notice connections that had been invisible to them, like a missing piece of pie on the table giving the appearance of a clock moving toward midnight ... in a painting about mortality. Possibilities for meaning and significance emerge. After three hours, the piece of art is not what the students expected.

This example is not likely to "sell you" on a similar practice. As you hopefully know by now, though, I am not interested in selling you anything; instead, I want to speak to you truthfully about things that matter.

Reading Scripture matters. Just like learning to "read" a piece of art, reading Scripture well starts with what we see. But just like my students standing in front of the paintings, seeing well takes time, effort, and humility on our part, because the word of God means to change us.

Eating the Word

There is a peculiar passage of Scripture that shows us what it means to really read Scripture. It is from the Book of the Prophet Ezekiel:

And when I looked, behold, a hand was stretched out to me; and behold, a written scroll was in it; and he spread it before me; and it had writing on the front and on the back. ... And he said to me, "Son of man, eat what is offered to you; eat this scroll, and go, speak to the house of Israel." So I opened my mouth, and he gave me the scroll to eat. And he said to me, "Son of man, eat this scroll that I give you and fill your stomach with it." Then I ate it and it was in my mouth as sweet as honey. Moreover, he said to me, "Son of man, all my words that I shall speak to you receive in your heart, and hear with your ears." (Ezekiel 2:9—3:3,10)

Let's see what is going on here. The prophet receives a scroll and is told to eat it. Maybe you have heard people say about a book that "I just couldn't put it down; I devoured it!" They were so engrossed in what they were reading that they "consumed" the written word until they had their fill. Ezekiel is told to consume like that. Ezekiel is scrolling, but not like we "scroll." To "eat" or "consume" something we read is quite different from a kind of passive, distant observance of the written word. We know what passive reading is like: That's how we "scroll," or skim something. But here, the prophet is told to go all in. The Lord tells him to give his full attention to this: Eat it up.

To fill your belly and digest what is written means to

ruminate on these words. Think about when you have a big meal: It takes time to digest what you have eaten. The food affects you as your body works on it. Now think about something a friend might say to you that sticks with you for a good or bad reason. You work it over in your mind, you keep thinking about it, you ruminate on it. So it is here with the word of God: Take it in, don't quickly forget it, work it over. To taste the sweetness of what you read (or hear) is to savor the sound of the words, find richness in the meaning. For Ezekiel, these words may not be the kind of thing he already likes, so he has to work to develop a taste for this sort of thing.

In the end, it is about receiving these words in your heart. That means to be changed by them. Where there is sorrow in these words, you, too, should experience sorrow. Where there is joy, experience joy. Where there is concern, be concerned. Where there is anger, be angry. If you think about empathic listening, where you share in the mood and emotions of a dear friend, then you get a sense for how the words and dispositions of what you read or hear affect you as the recipient.

What This Means for Our Reading

The Prophet Ezekiel is like one of my students standing in front of a piece of art. He immerses himself in what he encounters. He takes the time to notice things that weren't immediately apparent. He goes through ups and downs in the encounter, digesting what he takes in. And at the end of his encounter, he is not the same person he was when he started: The word has changed him in his mind, heart, and imagination.

To read Scripture well we must pay attention and open ourselves to being changed. The point of Scripture is not to give you what you want, but rather to give you the word of God: the one we need. He means to change us into his likeness, forming us to care about what he cares about, to feel sorrow for his sorrow, to rejoice in what he rejoices in. This is almost completely the opposite of our modern "scrolling," where we just breeze by looking for what we want and what pleases or entertains us.

It takes work to develop the skill for reading Scripture like this. But that work is well worth the effort because it prepares us to truly encounter the Lord, who speaks to us in and through Scripture. I offer you two quick suggestions for how to develop in the skill of reading Scripture.

First, engage your imagination. Over the course of two days, take one scene from the Gospels and spend at least thirty minutes each day picturing the scene and placing yourself in it. Taking the time to apply your imagination — building images, constructing a scene — allows your own creativity to be applied to the word of God. This work creates an impression on you, and that impression often stays with you. You will likely discover or "notice" things you didn't expect. The key here is to start with the biblical passage, read it over several times, then slowly imagine the scene, select a place within it, and see, hear, feel, smell, and taste what is happening. Stay with one episode for at least two days, and end each session with a one-page journal entry to record what you encountered.

Second, allow Scripture to remap your mind. For this, you need a Bible that includes annotations (references to other parts of Scripture, usually in the footnotes).[1] Choose a book of the Bible. Do not read it quickly. Instead, set out to read *at most* one chapter in a day. The key is to follow the annotations in the footnotes of your Bible to read other parts of Scripture that relate to a given verse or episode. For example, if you read the passion narratives in one of the Gospels, you will be regularly directed back to the psalms. Follow those references. Read the verse in the psalms that directly relates to the passage you read in the Gospel, then feel free to read more of the psalm. See how your understanding of the Gospel passage is being enriched, challenged, or stretched by what you are reading elsewhere. In this way you allow Scripture to educate you and create for you a mental map across multiple books. Be sure to keep a reading journal — this is hugely important.

These two practices may be used together, or you may practice one for a season, then the other for another season. These are, of course, not the only two practices, but they are good ones, and each one will incline you to start with what you see, then learn to see better, and ultimately be changed by the word of God who speaks to you.

14

How to Discern

You are not responsible for creating yourself. That's a countercultural statement in our day and age. It is now common to assume that you must construct your own identity and establish a personal brand or profile that asserts your uniqueness … just like everyone else.

Creating yourself might sound like freedom; really, it is an overwhelming burden. To have to make yourself in an image and likeness that you invent demands a degree of originality that is improper and impossible. It also leaves you subject to the virtually irresistible allure of influencers and powerbrokers, who drown you in proposal after proposal about how you can "do you," for yourself and by yourself.

That this myth of self-creation is in fact a lie is, itself, good news. That doesn't mean, however, that you are then passive in becoming who you were created to be. Rather, it means that you are truly free to become someone of substance, who is more than the sum of various preferences.

As Christians, we know that we have been *created* and *called*. Because God has created us, we do not have to achieve value — we begin as valuable in his image and likeness. And because God calls us, our lives are not about earning love but rather learning to give a free and generous response to the love of God poured out for us in Christ.

The Dominican preacher Timothy Radcliffe puts the matter this way: "A vocation, whether to be a priest or a religious, married or to practice a profession, goes against [the] grain. It is a witness to our hope that my life as a whole may have some sense. I do not just do things; I am called to be someone, and a vocation is part of saying who I am."[1]

Called to Be Someone

A priest wakes early on Tuesday to say his morning prayers and celebrate Mass for his parish. During breakfast, he receives a call that an elderly parishioner has been taken to the hospital and is not doing well. He arrives at the hospital room as family members start to gather. He administers the anointing of the sick to the old woman in the hospital bed. He leads the family in prayers. Then he waits with the family, as they await their loved one's death; he spends the better part of the day with them. The time he had planned to work on his homily for the weekend has been used up. Later that night, instead of reading for pleasure, he spends the hour working on his homily, before saying his night prayers and going to bed. He is tired from caring for his flock and tending to their needs.

A mother hears her child cry in the night. She goes to his room and finds what she expected: The child became ill. The mother has been here before, and she doesn't hesitate to pick him up to comfort and clean him. She lays him on her bed. She quickly strips her child's bed and starts the laundry. She returns to her child to again comfort him, though comforting him means that she will sleep uncomfortably the rest of the night. In the morning, she is tired from her interrupted sleep — tired from placing her child's needs above her own.

A teacher notices that one of her students has not been doing well in class. Even though the teacher is feeling burned out from a long month of teaching, she asks the student to stay behind to see what's going on. This is her lunch break, her one period of rest in the school day. The student eventually opens up. Things are not good for him at home, and it's affecting everything. The teacher spends her whole lunch break with him, then follows up with a phone call home after school. She makes a plan with her colleagues for offering support to this student. She prays for him that night. At the end of the day, she is tired from teaching many students and giving special attention to the one who needed her attention most.

These are images of what it means to respond to the call to "be someone." The priest, the mother, and the teacher made commitments long ago to serve and love in particular ways, and now in the midst of the day-to-day, they choose how to live out those commitments. In each instance, their own preferences are laid aside as they choose the duty of love.

Serving God for a Lifetime and for Today

There are times in our lives when we approach big decisions about who we will be. The challenge is to hear the voice of God and then take responsibility for making a commitment. But then in the day-to-day, we face the challenge of living as Christ's disciples in smaller decisions amid a variety of circumstances. In both the big decisions and smaller ones, we need to develop the spiritual skill of discernment: *How does Christ call me to commit myself as his disciple, and how do I serve him today?*

Many people turn to St. Ignatius of Loyola for guidance in discernment, and for good reason. His *Spiritual Exercises* guide people along a path of discernment, and his daily *Examen* helps them to enter into dialogue with God about their daily lives. The most important thing I found in following the way of Saint Ignatius, however, is a simple daily prayer that forces me to remember what is most important and beg God for that most important thing. The prayer goes like this: "My Lord and my God, I beg for the grace that all of my intentions, actions, and operations may be directed solely to the praise and glory of your divine majesty."

If you want to discern well, pray these words daily. Though it is a simple prayer, it is also a serious prayer. Discernment is about learning God's will and choosing to align your will with his. This prayer begs for the grace to do that. Intentions are what you mean to do; actions are what you do; and operations are how you do what you do. God must grant us the wisdom and the strength to put all that in alignment with his will, both in big commitments and in daily decisions. This prayer keeps us seeking the right thing in the right way, with God's help.

When it comes to discerning particular choices — especially life commitments — people like Saint Ignatius offer us helpful practices, such as imagining we are counseling someone else about this very choice, or imagining we are standing before the Lord at the end of our lives and looking back at this choice with him. The thing with these practices, though, is that they are not little tricks or techniques that suddenly make us capable of hearing God's voice and wanting to respond. Rather, as Saint Ignatius knew well, these practices build on long-standing Christian habits, which make true discernment possible. I want to close this chapter by mentioning four of these habits.

First: the habit of pondering and prayer. Dedicating time each day to being in silence with the Lord — say, thirty minutes — is crucial for getting used to listening for the Lord's voice. Especially for people like us who are immersed in a world of noise, the only way to *have* time to listen to God is to *make* time to be with him.

Second: the habit of forming our memory and imagination. There is never a question as to whether the way we happen to think and imagine is shaped by influences — we are all shaped by influences; it is part of our human nature. The real question is what influences will shape us most. As Christian disciples, we must be shaped by Scripture, the liturgy, and the sacraments. To be shaped by Scripture, we must regularly (at least weekly) study and pray with Scripture. We must participate in and learn to pray with the liturgy (including, if possible, the liturgy of the hours). And we must regularly receive the sacraments, growing in how we prepare for and respond to the sacraments.

Third: the habit of community. Regularly spending time with others, being attentive to the needs of others and acting on those needs, as well as allowing our own needs to be known to others who can care for us, is essential to the Christian life. Discernment is about discovering God's call for how we are to love, so becoming more perceptive of needs and skilled in performing acts of love equips us for true discernment. Along with this, finding and trusting a few key mentors keeps our discernment from becoming an exercise in individualism.

Fourth and finally: the habit of sacrifice and commitment. At the end of any process of discernment — no matter how good or thorough the practice is — you, as the one who discerns, come to a gap that only you can cross: the gap of trust and responsibility. God trusts each of us to take responsibility for being someone: to accept the consequences and fulfill our commitments. The way to prepare for being able to do that in big ways is to practice doing that in small ways. We should take even our small commitments seriously. Be wise in making commitments and then trustworthy in fulfilling those commitments. Those who develop the habit of breaking small commitments often break big ones, while those who honor small commitments are better prepared to keep big ones.

Maybe you recognize in these four practices many points of resonance with what you read in previous chapters. That is no accident. All throughout I have been writing to you about developing a Catholic character, and that character is the basis of true and faithful discernment. It is the development of character that bridges the gap between who you are and who you are called to become.

15

How to Sustain Friendships

Jesus' most impressive miracle was having twelve close friends in his thirties, with only one that betrayed him. That's not an original joke, yet it's still funny because it's true. You usually have far fewer friends when you are an adult. And having *close* friends and *lasting* friendships as an adult is harder still.

In an article for *The Atlantic*, Jennifer Senior says that she's "aged-out of the friendship-collecting business, which tends to peak in the tumbleweed stage of life. Instead," she continues, "I should be in the friendship-enjoying business, luxuriating in the relationships that survived as I put down roots."[1] There are a couple things worth noting in what she says. First, there is a shift in friendships as we age: It is easier and more natural to find and make new friends when you are younger, for myriad reasons. Second, when she speaks of "relationships that survived," it sounds like that's something that just happens: Some friendships live, some die. While there is some truth in that — due to circumstances such as location or having kids around the same time — what is left unsaid is that the friendships that endure are often the friendships you prioritize.

Some friendships end because of a bitter fight, or a change in values, or even outright betrayal. But most friendships end with a whimper. Nothing happens — it is just "that things stop happening between you," as Senior puts it. No sudden break, just silent drifting. This happens all the more during times of transition, such as when you move from high school to college, or college to the working world, or from one city to another, or from being single to married to married with children.

There are friendships so dear and enjoyable that you could never imagine them ending. And then you find yourself looking back over the past year or five years to see that you have hardly spent any time at all with the friend who was so dear to you. You miss your friend and you don't. You miss what you shared together and wish it was still there, but you spend your time on so many other things that you don't really feel the absence of that person, except maybe in fleeting moments of nostalgia.

There is, therefore, a radical difference between happening to have friends and *sustaining* friendships. The first is about chance; the second is about commitment. We should think about friendship more like a virtue: It is something you practice, grow in, and develop. You do not become virtuous by accident. In the same way, friendships require habits and actions. We cannot sustain all friendships forever — there is indeed a natural and even necessary winnowing of friendships that usually must occur as we grow older. It is not uncommon for most of us to have a large and growing list of "friends" on social media, yet there is a clear difference between the kind of friendship that Senior is talking about and I want to focus on here, and what these webs of loose connections mean in the digital world. Nurturing active friendships requires more than the easy linking that the digital world enables. In order to sustain the friendships that not only matter most but those we *want* to matter most, we have to foster intentionality, flexibility, and follow-through.

In this chapter, I want to share with you some of what I have learned through both study and experience about how to sustain friendships.

Prioritization

One of my best friendships started when I was a young adult, from my late twenties to mid-thirties. My friend Pete and I happened to work together for several years. We both loved playing basketball, and we played together often. There were a lot of reasons for us to spend time together.

Then circumstances changed. Pete started a big, time-consuming job, and he had to move on from the work that we shared together. My wife and I had more kids, and our older kids were in more activities that took up more of *our* time. Most of the reasons for us to spend time together expired. This was not as obvious a shift as going away to college or moving across the country, but the effect of these changes would be the same: We were about to drift — not because we didn't value the friendship; it is just that things had changed.

Fortunately, Pete and I realized that this was about to happen. Our response was really simple and really important. We decided that we would have lunch together every week. When we came up with this idea, one of us (I don't remember who) actually said, "If we don't make time to hang out, we're not going to." This was a friendship worth investing in, so we made it a priority. This commitment goes on the calendar before other things. Sometimes we have to miss a week or even two due to travel or other conflicts. But instead of always trying to "find time," we make time in advance, then we cancel when necessary. The default, in other words, is spending time together.

This is so obvious that I feel silly even mentioning it, but this is how priorities work. Priorities are the things that go on the calendar first. Priorities are not necessarily inalterable, but they do require a reason and an explanation for *not* holding to them. Pete and I have held to our weekly lunch date for several years now. If one of us moved to a different city, we would have to find another way to sustain the relationship. But I believe we would, and we would do so by making time spent in friendship a priority.

Focus

This will sound weird after what I just wrote, but a sure-fire way to put a friendship on the path toward its dissolution is to focus on the friendship itself. I think what happens is we idealize the friendship — we hold to the *idea* of being friends. True friendship, though, isn't about the cozy or reassuring feeling of being together. Rather, it is about desiring the other person's good.

Focusing on the other person's good means wanting what is best for the other person, acting in your friend's best interest, and even making sacrifices of time, effort, or preference to support your friend. It is nearly impossible for competitors to really be friends. Envy gets in the way, and envy eats at relationships from the inside. The commitment friends make to each other is to be there for each other and to support each other. To sustain a friendship, you have to make a commitment to be *for* your friend.

I think it is important to pray for friends. Praying for them means more than simply saying their name during prayer; rather, it means contemplating their good, their needs, their well-being, and interceding to God on their behalf. All of that costs you something, including the effort of displacing your focus from yourself. That is hard to do, but that cost is part of the cost of true friendship.

Favors

At least once I heard someone say, "If you want to make a friend, let someone do you a favor." That sounds counter-intuitive. It would seem that we make a friend when we do someone else a favor. But I think there is great wisdom here. We all want to know that we matter, and one of the best ways to know that is to know that we have mattered to someone else. So let someone else know that.

The few people that I count as my closest friends are people who are honest with me and ask me for advice and help. I think they count me as a close friend because I also turn to them when I am in need. We often learn how to love people by doing good things for them. That means that if we want to let people learn to love us, we have to let them do good things for us.

There is, of course, a line between allowing people to love us (or do good things for us) and becoming dependent on other people in an unhealthy way. Dependence is not bad in itself, but when we become disproportionately reliant on a friend or we expect them to always do what suits our interests, then something unhealthy develops for both parties in the friendship. There is a necessary prudence to friendship, such that we recognize and respect what it is appropriate to expect from some people but not from others. I can and should expect a higher level of investment in me from my wife and my very closest friends, as they should expect the same from me. But to expect the same from, say, my friends at work would often be out of place. This is probably all quite intuitive, but sometimes it is helpful to articulate the intuitive stuff so we can know it better.

Presence

It is easier now to be in touch with lots of people than ever before in history, and at the same time it is harder to be truly present to people than ever before. So here is something simple I have come up with:

Body > Voice > Writing > Texting

This means that being together in person — as in: bodily, in the same place at the same time — is the best kind of encounter. Encountering each other through voice — as in: by phone — is the next most personal and most real. Writing — as in: typically through the actual strokes of a pen, definitely in longer form as with letters — is next in line as a way of being present to each other. Last of all, short-form digital communication — as in: texting and the like — is not really a form of presence at all, but rather a way of keeping up chatter (it isn't bad, but it is no substitute for the more genuine thing). Whenever possible, privilege the more embodied form of presence. And above all, pray for each other (which means being present to each other in God).

There is no substitute in friendship for genuine presence. Sometimes, even for long periods of time, it is impossible to actually share time and space with a friend. The art, then, is to figure out how to be present to each other over distance. How do you make that person a part of your day and help them to make you a part of theirs? A little bit of presence every day is better than a whole lot of presence every once in a while. Likewise, connecting every week is better than a full week's vacation together once a year. The latter can be great and rejuvenating, but the former generates the sustaining power of friendships.

Stating the Obvious

In everything I have shared above, a basic assumption is that in order to sustain friendships, you have to *want* to sustain friendships. Friendships are not sustained by accident. I think, therefore, that periods of reflection are really important, especially as times of transition approach:

Which friendships are important to me?

Which friendships do I *want* to be important to me?

How do I — how do *we* — make sure those friendships not only survive but live and grow?

Asking questions like these is important to clarifying intentions. Once intentions are clear, making concrete, specific commitments becomes important for following through on those intentions. As we get older, I think we find that we have fewer friends by accident, leaving us with the opportunity to really cherish the friends we have on purpose.

16

How to Be Uncomfortable

We are like octopuses. We reach out for what we want. If one way of reaching out is closed to us, we find another way, and another, and another. Strong is our impulse to satisfy our urges. It takes concentrated effort to be free of these impulses. Actually, it takes practice and discipline. These are hard, hard things.

We like to be comfortable. No one likes to be uncomfortable. Our reflexes are bent toward comfort. The key is to retrain our reflexes, because always seeking after comfort makes us less than fully human.

Dorothy Day knew all about this. She slowly learned

to desire creating the kind of world where it was easier for other people to be good, to find joy, to be in community. Yet the thing that always got in the way of that desire was the urge to return to a place of comfort. To settle in and protect the little patch of happiness you presently have. To stop seeking what is truly great and beautiful for the sake of what is convenient, close at hand, and presently gratifying. Dorothy knew she was like an octopus — we all are:

> You can strip yourself, you can be stripped, but still you will reach out like an octopus to seek your own comfort, your untroubled time, your ease, your refreshment. It may mean books or music — the gratification of the inner senses — or it may mean food and drink, coffee and cigarettes. The one kind of giving up is not easier than the other.[1]

Dorothy didn't have anything against these things. Actually, she liked them. What she knew, though, is that craving any of these things too much, in the wrong way, or at the wrong time would stop her from promptly responding to the needs of others.

She *wanted* to care about the needs of others — to care about *their* good — but that desire did not always come easily, or without obstruction. Her own impulses got in the way. It is usually easiest to just go back to what you like and prefer and crave. But the line between enjoying these pleasures and becoming a slave to them grows faint if we always let ourselves reach for what we want when we want it.

We don't want what we don't like. Like many of us, Dorothy did not like uncleanliness or ugliness. Though she desired to seek the good of others, she did not like touching or being near what repulsed her.

Dorothy recalls "kissing a leper" — as she calls it — not once but twice, consciously. The first time occurred when she was giving alms to "a woman with cancer of the face." The woman tried to kiss Dorothy's hand. Rather than pulling away, Dorothy went against her own impulses. "The only thing I could do," she wrote, "was kiss her dirty old face with the gaping hole in it where an eye and nose had been." This was a direct act of love built upon years and years of trying to tame her impulses and do the hard thing when the hard thing was called for. "One gets used to ugliness so quickly. What we avert our eyes from one day is easily borne the next when we have learned a little more about love."[2] She learned that love is not first of all about great feelings; it is about actively willing the good of the other.

The second time she "kissed a leper" was much like the first. About both incidences she ends up saying, "We suffer these things and they fade from memory. But daily, hourly, to give up our own possessions and especially to subordinate our own impulses and wishes to others — these are hard, hard things; and I don't think they ever get any easier."[3] Why does this matter for us? Because we are no different than Dorothy. She liked things; we like things. She was called to a greater love; we are called to a greater love. She had to discipline her impulses in order to seek the better part, and so do we.

"You were not made for comfort. You were made for greatness." Benedict XVI said that, but it might as well have been Dorothy Day, or even Francis of Assisi. Greatness is found in seeking and acting on the good of others. That is where our own good is found. Addictions to comfort get in the way of what is good.

But *how* are we to get used to being uncomfortable? There are no shortcuts here. The only way is through practicing self-denial and practicing gratitude. Those sound like different things, but in truth they are two sides of the same reality.

Self-Denial

No matter what wealth you possess or what scarcity you endure in your life, everyone enjoys some comforts. There are probably some super hard-line people who would tell you that Christian life is only about suffering, and so any enjoyment is a sin. That's nonsense, and those people are delusional. But the truth of the matter is that every comfort, no matter how glamorous or relatively unglamorous, can slowly come to control you, if left unchecked. As a Christian you are called to be free of all attachments and ready to heed the Lord's call. If you cannot let go of a comfort, then you are not free.

This is why self-denial is so important. We are familiar with this mostly as a Lenten practice: Many people "give up" something they otherwise enjoy during Lent. These things that are given up are not, in themselves, bad or harmful, which is why giving them up is a sacrifice. If you gave up defacing property or mocking children, that's something different. That's about becoming a decent human being. But giving up something enjoyable — something that provides some comfort, which you like — is an act of self-denial. The point is not to give these things up forever. Rather, we give them up periodically so as to keep our attachment to these things in check, and to offer our small suffering to the Lord, or for the intention of someone else's well-being, or both.

Consider St. Francis of Assisi. He may very well be the patron saint of self-denial. He knew himself so well that he distrusted himself around comforts. He knew that he would very quickly get attached to things in the wrong way, and he would no longer be free. Once when he laid his head on a soft pillow, he noticed the comfort, and he immediately sought to free himself from the attachment. So he went outside to sleep with his head on a rock instead. When someone praised him, he would beg one of his brothers to insult him and remind him of his faults. He knew that he would quickly grow attached to praise, so he wanted to counteract it with a heaping dose of humility.

That might all sound crazy to you. It should. It sounds crazy to me. But don't get distracted and turned off by the intensity and seriousness of Francis's self-denial. Instead, heed the lesson. Francis desired the freedom of Christ so much that he would not let other attachments get in the way. We can pursue that kind of freedom by taking small steps. Even outside of Lent, choose one thing each month (or for one week each month) to just give up. Choose something enjoyable, which will make you a little uncomfortable when you give it up. This is the only way we *slowly* learn to love freedom more than we love all our little and big comforts.

Gratitude

Gratitude can be just as inconvenient and uncomfortable as self-denial. Do you recall that episode when Jesus cures ten lepers (see Lk 17:11–19)? Only one of them returns to give thanks. The others just go on their way, enjoying their new benefit. Their new benefit is quite grand: They were healed of leprosy, and thus restored to society, so they rush along to enjoy that. But one leper comes back and uses his new freedom to offer thanks to the one who healed him. That costs him something.

In another Gospel story, we encounter a woman who had been suffering from a blood disease for decades. This made her ritually impure, and thus she was excluded from social life. She was so desperate that she pushed her way through a crowd of people to lunge after Jesus as a last hope. She barely grazed the fold of his garment with her finger. But when she touched something that was touching him, she was healed. When Jesus turned around, the woman was lost in the crowd. She had gotten what she so desperately wanted, and she likely feared that she had done something improper. Yet, when Jesus called after the one who touched him, she came forward. She returned to the one who healed her, and that is the greater wonder. She looked him in the eye and heard him speak to her, personally. That is an exchange of gratitude (see Mk 5:25–34).

Gratitude is time-consuming, it is often inconvenient, and it costs us something. It is a form of self-denial. You could just enjoy the benefit you received, but instead you choose to suspend your enjoyment to say "thank you" to the one who gave you something. The regular practice of gratitude is a central practice of the Christian life. We become the kind of people we are created and called to be when we offer our gratitude to people who give to us, and ultimately to the Lord who gives all.

I close with a hard but undeniable truth: If being Christian does not cost you anything, then you are not really following Christ. The practices of self-denial and gratitude school us in the small and sometimes great costs of following Christ. They help us become fully human, rather than octopuses.

17

How to Be Mentored

It is all too easy to find someone who will tell you what you want to hear. It is much harder to find someone who, when necessary and out of concern for you, will tell you what you do not want to hear. We may think of ourselves as being mentored in either case, but seeking permission for what you already wanted is self-direction hiding under the cover of what looks like humility and obedience. Being truly mentored requires a willingness to wrestle with more, less, and other than what you would otherwise determine for yourself.

The Good Model
During the time in my life where I needed to learn how

to receive mentoring, I encountered a powerful model of such a relationship in a great work of literature I was reading for a college course. In *The Brothers Karamazov*, Alyosha seeks out direction from an elderly monk named Zosima. With his home life complicated and often clouded by suffering and sadness, Alyosha finds light, wisdom, and peace in Zosima. Alyosha goes to Zosima regularly, to learn from him and be formed by him. In fact, Aloshya wants to be a monk himself because, from his time with Zosima, he thinks becoming a monk would be "an ideal way out for his soul struggling from the darkness of worldly wickedness towards the light of love."[1] But in his final conversation with Zosima before the elder monk's death, Alyosha does not hear what he wants to hear. Instead, Zosima offers his mentee what he has come to see as the young man's true path and calling: "You will go forth from these walls to sojourn in the world like a monk."[2]

Alyosha wanted permission to leave his family's strife behind and enter the monastery. Zosima told Alyosha that his mission was to return to his family and serve them amid myriad complications and sufferings, and to do so with the freedom of one who has been formed in the monastic disciplines of obedience, fasting, and prayer.[3] It would have been very easy at this point for Alyosha to simply find someone who would tell him what he wanted to hear. But Alyosha did not take the easy path; instead, he wrestled with Zosima's direction. Zosima had earned Alyosha's trust, and Alyosha honored that trust by taking Zosima's counsel seriously. He allowed that counsel to shape his life.

The Bad Model

Just about the same time I was reading *The Brothers Karamazov*, I also saw (and then read) *A Man for All Seasons*, which is about St. Thomas More. Early on in that film (and play), the young Richard Rich comes to Thomas looking for direction in life. Richard wants to be an important man with a high and impressive office. Thomas, who knows Richard quite well, shows the young man that such an office would not be good for him. Instead, Thomas tells him, Richard would do well to become a teacher. Richard does not want to be a teacher, because he will not have a high status. This is precisely Thomas's point: Richard is lusting after status, not virtue and service.

It is hard for Richard to hear what Thomas has to tell him. Richard really wants Thomas to mentor him, but Richard wants to get his own way even more. So Richard aligns himself with another would-be mentor, who gives Richard what he wants, but neither knows nor cares for the young man himself. This leads to Richard's ruin — not in terms of his career, but in terms of his character. Richard becomes a man who will do anything for what he wants.

Alyosha Karamazov and Richard Rich began in similar situations but ended up very differently. Alyosha was willing to wrestle with his mentor's direction even to the point of adapting his own life plans. Richard, however, was so committed to the way he wanted to see things turn out for himself that he became impervious to the wise counsel of the mentor who tried to care for him. Alyosha became a man capable of sacrifice, while Richard became a man consumed by self-interest. Alyosha was willing to be mentored; Richard was not.

Pushing Back Against a World with Too Many "Mentors"

We are surrounded by "influencers." That is not a role that was suddenly invented on social media; there have always been influencers. What is different in our day is that the number of influencers or potential influencers who surround us has grown exponentially. Alyosha and Richard were, for the most part, limited in their influences — only the people around them could influence them. Because of our digital environments, the number of people who surround us is virtually infinite. We are bobbing along in an endless sea of influences.

The rise of the religious influencers is really no different than that of other media influencers. There are priests you've never met in person who offer guidance as if they were your pastor or spiritual director. There are alluring religious personalities who, with some media savvy, dispense popular wisdom and tutor large followings in spiritual and cultural matters. If we don't like what we hear from the pastor or teacher or guide who is proximate to us, then we can very easily find someone else who will delight and please us online. It is far from the case that every in-person influence is good and every online influence is bad. The point here is about the ease with which we can find other voices whenever we want, which is easier today than ever before.

When we swap out our mentors too often, or when we just surf around for what we want to hear or for a voice that engages us, then we are doing something more than seeking counsel. We are actually accustoming ourselves to shopping for influences. It is the shopping that grabs hold of us. We get buyer's remorse for taking in some influence the moment it becomes unpleasant, so we go in search of another influence to buy. Buyers beware, indeed. We ought to be on guard, suspicious of an environment where so many influencers or would-be mentors are vying for our attention with advice so easily consumable. Ease is the enemy of depth.

That brings me to the three necessary practices in how to be mentored, which I hope will be helpful to you.

The first necessary practice is to limit and guard your influences. Some of us like the *feeling* of being mentored more than actually being mentored. What I mean is that it is, at times, enjoyable to have someone else take an interest in our well-being and offer us direction. It is so enjoyable that, for example, I have seen quite a few college students collect "mentors" like patches for a letterman jacket. But what this really does is drown out the voices of those who are actually in the position to offer the most honest, knowledgeable, and considerate counsel. Alyosha spent time with Zosima, and Zosima came to know Alyosha quite well. If Alyosha had five more mentors whom he counted as equal to Zosima, then Zosima's counsel would have been relativized and diluted. We can attach ourselves to these "would-be mentors" in person and online, allowing more and more voices to swirl around our heads. That is a recipe for both confusion and, more likely, self-direction: opting for the voice who tells you what you like best. The key is intentionally limiting your primary mentors. Invest in those few relationships so that those people can invest in you.

The second necessary practice is twofold: consistency and honesty. To allow someone to be a mentor to you, you must communicate with them regularly. It is easier to go to mentors only when you need something, but that diminishes how well the mentor can mentor you. Staying in consistent contact with a mentor — even to the point of scheduling out in advance regular meeting times — adds stability and familiarity to the relationship. This obviously requires that the communication be as honest as possible. A mentoring relationship is not a relationship among equals — as mentee, the focus is on you. A good mentor places his or her primary attention on the other person, listening closely and acting deliberately. Sometimes it is really hard to be honest with a mentor because you want to keep up appearances, or you don't want to disappoint, or you want to pick and choose what to share. The more honest you are with your mentor, the more the focus can be on who you really are instead of who you appear to be.

The third and final practice I share is threefold: Choose intentionally, reflect deeply, follow up thoughtfully. Very rarely are we assigned mentors in life; instead, we typically have to seek out our mentors. We should therefore choose our mentors intentionally. Whom can I trust? Who is capable of guiding me? Whose virtues and character are worthy of imitation? It is even okay to "interview" mentors, to see whether they would be willing to mentor you, whether they can commit to sharing time and wisdom with you, and how they would do so.

Sometimes potential mentors are easier to identify when you are younger, such as when in high school or on a college campus that has designated ministers. Most of the time in adult life, though, potential mentors are not so obvious. In the workplace, is there someone (perhaps not your direct boss) who not only does their work well but maintains good relationships with others and seems to foster balance and integrity? Are there people in your parents' generation — such as the parents of your friends or friends of your parents — who live the kind of life you would like to emulate, even if not in every particular detail like their field of work or marital status? In your parish, are there regular, solid parishioners who are dedicated to the life of faith and to the community, whom you might benefit from spending time with and learning from their core commitments and practices? Just as finding new friends in adult life is not as easy as during school years, identifying mentors is also more challenging as an adult. But with intentionality and persistence, some of the best and most formative mentors can be discovered when you are an adult searching for good mentors among other adults, especially those with more life experience than you.

Following from that initial intentionality in seeking out mentors, the next form of intentionality is found in reflecting deeply on what you share with a mentor and what they offer back to you. I recommend keeping a journal where you can prepare for conversations with a mentor *and* reflect on your mentoring discussions afterward. This is the kind of work that allows you to make the best use of — and take as seriously as possible — the mentoring relationship.

Reflecting on your conversations prepares you to fulfill the third form of intentionality, which is following up thoughtfully. Let's consider, for example, if after Alyosha received Zosima's instruction and seriously grappled with it, Alyosha discerned, to the best of his ability, to pursue a different path from the one Zosima advised. The thoughtful follow up for Alyosha would, in that case, entail coming back to Zosima to talk with him about why he is choosing a different path (or in this case, since Zosima was dying, to talk with someone else about this). The mentor may, of course, respond and even disagree, but any mentor worth his weight in salt will appreciate, admire, and respect the free decision of his mentee when the mentee "shows his work," so to speak, or shares the reasons for his decision.

We are not meant to find our paths alone. You and I both need mentors to help us along the way. A biblical proverb reads: "He who walks with wise men becomes wise, / but the companion of fools will suffer harm" (Prv 13:20). Fools tell us what we want to hear, while those who are wise tell us what we need to hear. If we follow only what we want, we become like the fools. If we are willing to accept what we need, we are wise and become wiser.

18

How to Mentor

I had had a conversation like this a hundred times be-fore. A student came to my office because she wanted to talk about something going on in her life. She began: "I have a hole in my heart, and I need to take care of it."

I responded with empathy: "I'm so sorry. That sounds hard." From her first line I gathered that some love interest had broken her heart, or some friendship had fallen apart, or some family relationship was on the rocks. She was heartbroken; there was a hole in her heart. I had had a conversation like this a hundred times before.

I took on a compassionate silence so she could tell me as much as she wanted to. She went on telling me

137

about this hole in her heart. I kept listening, nodding along and waiting to hear who pierced her heart and how.

But as she kept talking, what she was saying did not exactly follow the kind of script I expected. Instead of talking about a relationship, she was talking about doctors' visits. Instead of talking about her sadness and sorrow, she was talking about her symptoms. Instead of talking about restoring her emotional or psychological health, she was talking more about her physical health.

And then it hit me: "Oh, wait … you mean … you actually, physically have a *hole in your heart*?!"

"Yes," she said, "a real hole … in my heart … and I need to take care of it."

She got how I totally missed what this was all about. She laughed. I laughed. Then we got back to the matter at hand, but this time I was really listening, because I had never had a conversation like this before.

Turning into a Mentor

The originality of that one mentoring conversation is not the exception but the rule. Even if, to a mentor, a conversation seems familiar because you have had ones like it with other people in the past, that familiarity is limited, and you must let go of it. Each person you mentor is never in any way just a repetition of other people you have mentored. This person before you is an original. Their situations are original. Their life is original. The best mentors are those who have become expert in recognizing the originality of the person and their situation even as the mentor draws on past experience to do so.

The best mentors are *not* those who, like me, assume they know what is going on too soon because they have had a hundred conversations like this before. Because they haven't. In my situation, I hadn't. Even if my mentee had come to talk about her broken heart rather than the actual hole in her heart, she and her situation would have been original. It was about *her* heart.

I am writing to you about mentoring because mentoring is one of the most important responsibilities of adult life. It is also one of the necessary and essential facets of mature Christian discipleship — a way in which disciples give as they themselves have received. You may consider yourself more someone who needs to *be mentored* than someone who is called to mentor others. But there is no clear commencement date separating the former from the latter. For many of us it just sort of happens: Suddenly, other people look to us for guidance. Somehow, we have something to pass on, our support matters, and our advice carries weight. Far too many people turn away from this responsibility of mentoring. I am writing to you about how to mentor because (if I can "should" you for a moment) you *should not* be one of those people who turns away from mentoring but rather someone who turns toward it.

This chapter — like all the chapters in this book — is not primarily about "why" but rather "how" to mentor.

I hope you will just grant that the willingness and availability to mentor is in keeping with stronger character
and true maturity. With that, then, let me share with you
some thoughts about the "how" of mentoring.

From Listening to Rejoicing

Let's make a plain thing plain: There is no such thing
as a good mentor who is not a good listener. All good
mentoring depends on and builds from good listening,
careful listening, even creative listening. In the story I
shared above, I thought I was there with my mentee and
ready to listen, but I wasn't. I was assuming too much,
interpreting too soon, and falling into a certain kind of
script while expecting my mentee to do the same. That's
not listening, and I was not yet ready to mentor, guide,
and support her well.

The first duty of a mentor is to prepare to listen fully
and without prejudice. You may remember that in chapter 8, I recalled what Simone Weil said about loving your
neighbor, which is that love of neighbor always begins
from one question: "What are you going through?" For
a mentor, that question should shape your fundamental disposition, because it is a question about the other
person and their situation. It is about *them,* and they get
the first word. The mentor's first priority is to listen and
listen well.

I don't think listening well just happens in the moment, as in when the other person is speaking or otherwise communicating. Good and deep listening happens

afterward, too. I have learned from experience that I sometimes *really* hear what was said (or trying to be said, or hoping to be said, or begging to be said) sometime afterward, after things have settled into my mind. A wise practice for a wise mentor is therefore to keep a mentoring journal, or something like that. On the one hand, it is a way to take notes (after the fact) of conversations or other interactions with someone you are mentoring so that you can recall those experiences well later on, when memory fades. On the other hand, it is a way to reflect on what has been shared, to make connections that were not at first readily apparent, and to engage in some "creative listening" where you can start to think with your mentee and maybe even open up new areas of understanding or growth that they haven't considered.

Good mentors make their wisdom and experience available to their mentees, for their mentees' benefit. Good *Christian* mentors do that, too, but they also actively seek divine wisdom and guidance for their mentees' benefit. In other words, Christian mentors pray for those whom they mentor. If mentoring is about seeking the other person's good and fulfillment, then praying for a mentee is offering their needs and their growth to the One who knows them best and cares for them absolutely. The good Christian mentor also prays for wisdom and humility in themselves, so that they can mentor well and truly become a student of their mentee: learning what they are going through, studying what is good for them, becoming more attuned to the originality of their life.

In prayer, a good Christian mentor might ask the Lord to help them see what exactly is the good their mentee is called toward. You ask to learn to see the knots and tangles that are part of the other person's desires and relationships. You might petition the Lord to help you see what you have not seen but need to see, or what the mentee has not seen in their own life but may grow to see.

I remember in the novel *Gilead* by Marilynne Robinson how her main character, John Ames, who is a pastor, talks about his love for the ministry of reconciliation. Not only does he love helping people name and heal from their sins, but he also loves working to see the ways in which people influence one another and how their lives are tied up together. He talks about it in terms of planetary motion. If you imagine the earth orbiting the sun, you can fairly easily recognize (even if you can't "see" it) that the sun exerts gravitational force upon the earth. You might also think about how the earth exerts gravitational force upon the moon, which orbits around the earth. But then you might think about how the moon is caught in the gravitational pull of the sun and the earth alike, so that the moon feels the pull of the sun directly, the earth directly, and the sun indirectly through the earth. You can keep going like this with every planet and every moon exerting force on one another, whether directly or indirectly. John Ames's point is that to see the real drama in any person's life — especially how God's grace acts upon them — requires learning to see, with greater and greater sensitivity and skill, the way in which those close to them and those not so close to them influence, shape, bless, curse, strengthen, and harm them, and how they do that to others, and how everyone does that for and to one another both directly and indirectly.

That is all a very long way of trying to explain my point: When you are a mentor who is seeking the good for another person, you cannot simply focus on the other person as if they were an isolated individual. No one person is just a single, simple narrative. Truly seeing a person you are mentoring is the ongoing activity of learning to see them better, more fully, in all their wondrous and messy complexity. A Christian mentor ought to pray for the eyes to see, the ears to hear, the mind to know, and the heart to cherish more and more the *full* person they are mentoring.

Love Is Patient, Love Is Kind

Mentoring requires patience and kindness. Those are the first two things that Saint Paul identifies with love in 1 Corinthians 13. Patience is twofold: First, it is about withholding judgment (at least premature judgment); and second, it is about giving the benefit of the doubt, offering the gift of time, opening up the space of possibility. It can be tempting as a mentor to move your mentee along at your own preferred pace — and indeed, sometimes mentees need to be nudged, urged, and prodded — but the good of the other person does not conform itself to our timelines.

And yet while waiting and exercising patience — whether for the mentee's decision about a matter, or development in virtue, or growth in some capacity — incline that time and space of waiting to the mentee's good. In other words, act on behalf of what is good for your mentee, what is nourishing or strengthening. Be kind. Sometimes those ways of being kind are obvious: Write the letter of recommendation that will help them, make the call or send the introductory email that gives them the connection they need, show up to support them when they do the thing they do. Other times, though, those ways are not so obvious, and you just have to do the kind and generous thing for them even when there doesn't seem to be the obvious occasion for it: Send the encouraging note, give the small gift, offer the compliment that is true and honest.

The Music of Mentoring

As I have thought about mentoring, especially in terms of those who have mentored me and those whom I have mentored, I have come to think in terms of music. Mentoring is about finding the music that someone else can dance to well, rather than trying to force your own taste in music on someone else. Think about the difference there. Mentoring is not shaping someone else according to your own preferences and preferred script, and it is definitely not about micromanaging another person. What mentoring is about is helping to shape the freedom and responsibility of another person, in the way appropriate to your particular relationship and what they need or seek from you.

The point of mentoring is that the other person should become more and more free, more and more responsible. Mentoring is about playing an important part in helping someone else to grow and flourish — to dance, if you will, in the way that they are created and called to dance. You might even think of mentoring as helping other people to someday become good mentors themselves, who may share their own wisdom, experience, and support with generosity, patience, and kindness.

Finally, as a mentor you ought to let your mentee be a joy to you. If you do not find joy in the well-being of the other person, then pray — indeed, beg — for the grace to delight in them. If joy will not come, then help them find another mentor in your stead. Yet if joy does come from this relationship — as it should and often does — then thank God for that gift. The person who has trusted you is an expression of God's own generosity toward you.

19

How to Grieve

The good thing about not caring about something is that you don't care when it's gone. Actually, that's not a good thing at all. Maybe it's convenient and easier not to care, but we are created to care about things and especially about people. The risk of pain in losing who and what we care about is the cost of being the kind of people we are supposed to be: people who care.

I think there are really only three kinds of people: those who have experienced heartbreak, those who have not yet experienced heartbreak but will, and those who avoid heartbreak at all costs. The first two are separated by circumstance, the last by apathy or stoicism or fear. Of course, we all want to be happy; in fact, we are created for and called to unending happiness, but not at the expense of avoiding suffering. Part of our growth and development toward becoming fully human is found in learning how to suffer well, which includes learning how to grieve. Grief is the natural, human response to losing something or someone we love. Without love, there is no grief.

You may already know exactly what I'm talking about because you have experienced the kind of suffering for which there is no "afterward" when things go back to "normal." That is the kind of suffering where "normal" itself changes. Or you may not know this personally, and if not, it is really hard to imagine what that might be like. Whether you have or have not suffered in this deep and life-altering way, I think we share a common duty: to prepare to become the kind of people who learn how to bear with loss rather than avoid loss. That sounds unappealing, like a total downer of an idea, yet the truth is that we are created for more than we often expect or desire for ourselves. We are created for the great joy and privilege of loving, and for being the kind of people who can and will bear the cost of love.

I have suffered and grieved in my life, but it is entirely possible that you have suffered and grieved more. It goes without saying that I am nowhere near the person who has suffered and grieved the most, so I am no real expert on this stuff from experience. But as I have tried to do throughout this book, I want to draw both from my experience and, even more, from what I have learned and come to believe to try to tell you the truth about grief. There are four things I want to share with you about how to grieve.

Grieve Slowly

So much of our modern lifestyles is about staying on schedule. We pack our days with an ever-increasing number of things to do, things to glance at, and things to worry about. We hate getting behind, we fear being behind, and yet we are constantly behind. We live in environments where progress is everything, where speed and efficiency are revered. We are even encouraged to treat losses in this manner: Deal with them quickly and move on. Don't get bogged down, don't dwell on things, don't stop moving.

Grief protests against the tyranny of progress. Rushing means not taking things or people seriously, and grief emerges from the recognition that what or who you have lost does indeed matter. If they didn't matter, you wouldn't feel sorrow. Letting the pain of grief rest with you is how you honor what or whom you have lost.

Practically speaking, grieving slowly requires changes to what and how you live on a day-to-day basis. During a period of grieving, you should intentionally declutter your schedule, you should *not* submerge yourself under one distraction after another, and you might develop some new practices for how to give yourself the time and space to honor your grief: journaling, periods of silence throughout the day, a retreat, creating art, talking with a confidant or mentor.

Nothing is sadder than a life where nothing matters. Give yourself time to grieve because the people and experiences in your life *do* in fact matter.

Grieve Deeply

Clichés are for the shallows. "Everything happens for a reason" distorts the truth and promises an easy out for the hard things. For those of us who believe in God and entrust him with our lives, it is true that God abides with us in all things and that he will carry all things to a good end in him, if we will but let him. But that doesn't mean that there is a reason for violence, or betrayal, or cancer, or death. God does not respond to such things with an explanation — "here's why this happened, here's the reason." Instead, God answers with action: God moves near to us in our sorrow and shares in it. The Incarnation is nothing if not that. "Everything happens for a reason" is a distortion of that exceedingly more profound and marvelous truth.

"God must have wanted another angel in heaven." "If that school didn't want you, then they don't deserve you." "You're better off without him." There is usually some kernel of truth in responses like these, but that kernel is wrapped in the message to try to let this thing glance off you. Now, of course, we can become paralyzed by grief when it becomes the only thing in our lives, but trying to let things glance off you rather than letting a loss feel like a loss and feeling the sting of that loss deeply makes us into shallow people. One antidote to the ease of clichés is simply saying, "This sucks." Sorry for the language, but "this stinks" just doesn't quite cut it. Grieving deeply requires saying and allowing yourself to feel that some things do, in fact, suck.

One non-clichéd saying that has stuck with me over the years is from Léon Bloy, who said that "there are places in the heart that do not yet exist, and into them enters suffering, that they might exist." That's a hard thing to grasp. I think you only grasp it by allowing suffering to enter your heart. Only then do we discover how the suffering and grief that we take to heart strangely, almost miraculously, make our hearts grow larger. We become more rather than less capable of compassion, and therefore of love.

Grieve Openly

I mean this in two senses. The first sense is this: Do not grieve in shame or in secret. It is a distinctly (and unhealthy) modern thing that those who grieve are more or less expected to grieve in private. Public mourning has become taboo. This is nonsense, and it is completely inhumane.

That does not mean that we are to make a show or a spectacle of our grief; instead, it means that we should never feel pressure to keep our grief secret. Share your grief with friends, coworkers, neighbors, each in a way appropriate to your relationship with them. If you feel that you have to keep your grief private, then I mean this in all seriousness: That is the devil working. The devil always leads us away from the fullness of our humanity. Be human: Grieve openly.

The second sense of grieving openly is about doing something with your grief. Open your grief up. I learned about this from Saint Augustine. Earlier in his life, he had a friend who was very dear to him, who Augustine says was inseparable from him for over a year. Whatever the fourth-century term for "besties" was, that's what they were. Then this friend died, unexpectedly. Augustine says that then "black grief closed over my heart."[1] What he means is that his whole world locked up around him. All he did was spend his time seeing and thinking about how his friend was not there and how his own life was now only marked by this loss. He didn't do anything with his grief; he just sat in it and let it consume him.

Now that sounds strange coming after what I just said in terms of grieving deeply. It seems like Augustine grieved very deeply, and indeed he did. But grieving deeply does not mean you cannot or should not grieve openly. Augustine shows us this later in his life, when his mother, Monica, died. *No one* was dearer to him than his mother, and he grieved no one's death more deeply than Monica's.[2] The difference by this point in his life, though — after he had become a Christian, by the way — is that he risked doing something with his grief. First, he prayed about it, offering his pain to God, asking for God's healing. Second, he prayed for his mother, begging God to forgive her whatever sins she had and to take her into his love. Third and finally, he did what his mother asked him to do before she died: He remembered her at the altar — that is, he offered his pain and prayers for her with Jesus' offering in the Eucharist. This is not some kind of little religious trick, and it is anything but magic. He did not suddenly feel all better. He continued grieving, but he did something with his grief. He opened it to God and, as a matter of fact, opened it to others in writing about it. His grief was both deep and open.

Grieve Communally

Just as there are two sides to grieving openly, there are two sides to grieving communally. First, be open to sharing your grief with others. This can be a really hard thing to do, but it is absolutely necessary. Yes, this is for your own good, but you know what … it is also for other people's good. In sharing your grief with others, you are doing *them* a favor: You are giving them the opportunity to become more fully human, to be compassionate, to be who and how *they* are created to be.

One of the greatest obstacles to mercy is the way in which we hide our sufferings from one another. By doing that, we deprive others of the chance to be merciful. Being merciful is the way to be fully human. Sharing your grief with others gives them the chance to be merciful. Not everyone will respond well, and no one will respond perfectly; still, make it possible for others to join you in your suffering. Especially in those times when you cannot control much else, this is something you can control: sharing your grief with others.

The other side of grieving communally is about when *other people* grieve, rather than you. When it comes to other people, you cannot determine whether or not someone else will be afflicted by grief. What you can always decide, though, is whether or not another person grieves *alone*. Do not let others grieve alone. You can decide to join them in their grief (after all, grief usually feels very lonely). You can choose to pay the cost of loving them. You can bear what is not yours *as if* it were yours. You can spend time with them, weep with them, listen to them, console them, pray with and for them, offer small sacrifices for them, and even offer big sacrifices for them. You can let their pain affect you. This is not the easy path; it hurts. But it is a pain you choose out of love. It is part of the cost of being fully human. It is a serious but glorious price to pay.

20

How to Find Joy

One of the most joy-filled things I've ever read is a letter that begins "I have a brain tumor."[1] The author was in her early thirties. She was a wife to a devoted husband, a mother to four young children, a friend to really good friends. Her diagnosis was terminal, and she knew it. She knew she may not live to see her thirty-fifth birthday, and she was quite sure she would not make it to forty. Beth Haile was dying, and she was joyful.

This is not to say that she was happy about dying. She loved her life. She loved her husband, she adored her children, she cherished her friends. She liked the work that she had been trained to do. She enjoyed simple pleasures. She did not want to leave this world, nor did she want her husband, and especially not her children, to be without her. She did not want to miss what she was now certain she would miss. Happiness, it turns out, is not the same as joy. She was joyful even though she wasn't happy about everything.

Four years before her letter about her brain tumors, Beth wrote another letter about reprioritizing her life.[2] After a year of prayer, guidance, and discernment, she decided to rebalance what she had come to see as a work-life *imbalance*. She realized she couldn't will all possible goods, so she made intentional choices about what to place first in her life, what came next, and so on. By the time her brain tumors were discovered (as she writes in her open letter, she actually had two tumors), she had been living into the renewed commitments she had made for a few years. She found joy, even though she sacrificed many things to live out these new commitments.

One year after she wrote her letter about her brain tumors, Beth Haile died. She died with sorrow for the separation from her husband and children and friends and this world, and she died with gratitude for it all. Happiness is a fickle thing, but joy is wide enough to hold sorrow and gratitude.

I've read Beth's letters many times. She wrote them for a public audience. I have come to see Beth as a witness to joy. She found joy in this life, and she awaited the joy of the life to come. Those are not separate joys; it is the same joy. The joy that began in her here will be complete in the hereafter. That is the Christian hope.

I do not tell you about Beth to scare you. This is not a "you might die tomorrow" ploy. Had Beth been miraculously cured, were she still living, if she was at home now with her husband and children, I would still consider her a witness to joy. The joy was there as much in the earlier letter as it was in the later one. She had made the decision to leave happiness to find joy. There were things she liked in the way her life was before she reprioritized, and she had to leave some of those things behind. Leaving those things behind hurt. But she was willing to heed a deeper calling, to move beyond what had become comfortable and customary, and to open herself to a fullness of life. Her early death is not what made her life full. Rather, her words as she approached her early death showed the rest of us what the fruits of living life fully are. She was free to embrace sorrow for the things that were sorrowful, and she was free to exude gratitude for the things that made her grateful. She let us glimpse what joy is.

At the end of this book, I now write to you about how to find joy. I do not think I can say anything better than what Beth testifies to. The main thing is this: You have to be willing to leave happiness to find joy.

The Sacrifice of Joy

I have sometimes asked students I teach who they think was the most obvious saint of the twentieth century, if they could only name one person. By far the most popular response is Saint Teresa of Calcutta. It seems that here is a woman who was just born to be a saint. She has almost become a type — as in, someone could be called "a Mother Teresa." Something like that would mean that the person is a living saint. We might assume that she just had a gift for holiness, like she was just made that way. While I do not at all discount the way in which grace moved in her life, I also want to tell you something that I have discovered about her from studying her, praying with her, and listening to what other people had to say about her: Like Beth Haile after her, she too left happiness to find joy.

Mother Teresa rarely spoke about her childhood, but the few times that she did she always said that she came from a very happy home. Her father taught her and her siblings how to welcome people, especially poor people, into their home to share what they had, while her mother taught them how to go out from their happy home to tend to the needs of people in their community. She learned early that her happy home was a place into which to welcome people, and out of which to serve people. When as a teenager she discerned a call to join a religious community that served children in faraway India, the cost of following that call was leaving her happy childhood home behind forever. She went.

The pain of leaving home brought Sister Teresa to the joy of educating the Bengali poor in India. She initially taught history and geography alongside catechism, and when she professed her perpetual vows as a Sister of

Loreto in 1937, now-Mother Teresa also served as religious superior of one of Loreto's schools. She was very happy. In fact, even later in life, she said that living as a Sister of Loreto was the happiest that she had ever been. But soon she came to learn of people even poorer than the ones she was serving in her schools, and soon after that she discerned a very clear call from the Lord to go and serve these "poorest of the poor." She was happy in Loreto, but she did not cling to her own happiness. Instead, she began the process of seeking permission from her religious superiors to follow this specific calling. And when, after two years, she was granted permission from her religious superiors and her bishop, she left Loreto behind forever.

The pain of leaving Loreto brought Mother Teresa and the Missionaries of Charity who followed after her into the joy of loving the poorest of the poor, first on the streets of Calcutta and then across the world. For those dying on the streets with no one to care for them, Teresa brought them into homes where they could be cared for, respected, and accompanied to death if they could not be healed. For those whose misery was hidden in forgotten places, Teresa went out of her homes to find them, to keep them company, and to bring them the light of love. She took what she learned about a happy home as a child and gave that gift to those who had no home of their own.

She who left happiness to find joy became, for others, a witness to joy. One man who bore witness to her joy was a very accomplished journalist named Malcolm Muggeridge. He went to India to see what Mother Teresa was all about. Slowly, he began to marvel at her and her fellow missionaries; but even more, he started to marvel at the people they were serving. In one very telling passage in a book he wrote about his experiences, he said this:

> Accompanying Mother Teresa, as we did, to these different activities for the purpose of filming them — to the Home for the Dying, to the lepers and unwanted children, I found I went through three phases. The first was horror mixed with pity, the second compassion pure and simple, and the third, reaching far beyond compassion, something I have never experienced before — an awareness that these dying and derelict men and women, these lepers with stumps instead of hands, these unwanted children, were not pitiable, repulsive or forlorn, but rather dear and delightful; as it might be, friends of long standing, brothers and sisters.[3]

Do you see how even in this one account, Malcolm himself is leaving something settled for something new? He was afraid of deformity, afraid of sickness, afraid of poverty. He was content in his clean and orderly life. Following Mother Teresa brought him to what he feared. But there, in the midst of those in need of compassion, *he* started to change because he didn't run away. He saw their need for compassion, and he felt the compassion himself. And yet, he was changed even more profoundly: He began to delight in the very people who previously repulsed him. *He* felt companionship with them, *he* delighted in them, *he* found joy.

There is no joy without risk.

Where to Set Our Hearts

We routinely fail to seek after what we are meant for. We cling to our lesser pleasures, our safeties, our conveniences and routines and habits. We neglect the call to joy.

C. S. Lewis wrote about this in one of his most famous little essays, which was really a sermon. He said,

> It would seem that Our Lord finds our desires not too strong, but too weak. We are half-hearted creatures, fooling about with drink and sex and ambition when infinite joy is offered us, like an ignorant child who wants to go on making mud pies in a slum because he cannot imagine what is meant by the offer of a holiday at the sea. We are far too easily pleased.[4]

There is a lot of wisdom in that. This is about God, and how God creates us — what God creates us for. We are not intended to turn off our desires; in fact, our desires are meant to become enflamed. Settling for too little stops us from desiring more — for ourselves and for each other. We are made for the kind of joy that Beth Haile tasted, a joy that confounds those of us who have not experienced it. The joy that Mother Teresa sought, which Malcolm Muggeridge experienced when he followed her, is not a greater joy than what is meant for us. It is the same joy. It is more than we tend to imagine. It may not even be what we think we want, but our dissatisfaction with everything short of that kind of joy is an indication that we are made to be not half-hearted, but full-hearted creatures.

I do not have much else to write to you about the "how" of finding joy, other than to say what I have already said: We have to be willing to leave happiness to find joy. That will look different in your life than in mine, but the challenge is the same. It was the same for Beth, the same for Teresa, and the same for Malcolm. The challenge is leaving the comfort of happiness; the reward is the joy of Christ.

If you cannot believe in Christ, then practice moving the way people like Beth and Mother Teresa moved. Be not afraid to sacrifice happiness when necessary for the sake of joy. Go toward those in need. Make the sufferings of others your own. Rejoice in other people's good. If you do that, you will already be moving in the ways of God. Sometimes we get to belief by way of action, even if it takes a long time to get there.

The truth is this: There is no joy without God. That

is *the* truth, and all along I have wanted to tell you the truth. I want you to know that I am not as joyful as I should be. Pray that I may grow in joy, which means that I may give my life over more and more to God, to the ways of God. And I will pray the same for you.

Notes

Chapter 3: How to Study and Work

1. Quoted in Cal Newport, *Deep Work: Rules for Focused Success in a Distracted World* (New York: Grand Central Publishing, 2016), 158.

2. This ninety-minute rule is noted in a number of places, including in Newport, 97 and 112.

Chapter 4: How to Pray — Part 1

1. Raymond of Capua and Lamb, *The Life of St. Catherine of Siena*, 63; see also Catherine of Siena, *The Dialogue*, 56.

Chapter 6: How to Pray — Part 3

1. Quoted in "Introduction" to Saint Teresa of Ávila, *The Interior Castle*, trans. Kieran Kavanaugh and Otilio Rodriguez (New York: Paulist Press, 1979), 40; see also St.

Teresa of Ávila, *The Way of Perfection*, ed. E. Allison Peers (Mineola, NY: Dover Publications, 2012), 135.

2. This is from a letter Teresa wrote on October 9, 1581. See Teresa of Ávila, *The Collected Letters of St. Teresa of Ávila*, trans. Kieran Kavanaugh, vol. 2 (Washington, DC: ICS Publications, 2007), 460.

Chapter 7: How to Begin to Love Your Neighbor

1. Pietro Molla and Elio Guerriero, *Saint Gianna Molla: Wife, Mother, Doctor* (San Francisco: Ignatius Press, 2004), 63–64.

Chapter 8: How to Actually Love Your Neighbor

1. If you are interested in more on this interpretation of the parable of the good Samaritan, see Henri de Lubac, *Catholicism: Christ and the Common Destiny of Man* (San Francisco: Ignatius Press, 1988), 204–205.

Chapter 10: How to Have Sex

1. Favale, *Into the Deep*, 34.

2. For more on this understanding of the procreative dimensions of marriage and sexual union, see the *Catechism of the Catholic Church*, especially nos. 2335, 2367.

3. I am always reachable at leonard@leonardjdelorenzo.com or through my website at leonardjdelorenzo.com.

Chapter 11: How to Be Eucharistic — Part 1

1. Thérèse of Lisieux, *Story of a Soul: The Autobiography of St. Thérèse of Lisieux*, trans. John Clarke (Washington, DC: ICS Publications, 1996), chapter 8.

Chapter 12: How to Be Eucharistic — Part 2

1. Benedict of Nursia, *The Rule of St. Benedict*, ed. Timothy Fry (New York: Vintage Books, 1998), 3.

2. Ibid., 5.

3. Joseph Putz, *My Mass* (Westminster, MD: Newman Press, 1948), page number not available.

4. Benedict XVI, *Deus Caritas Est*, no. 14.

Chapter 13: How to Read Scripture

1. Personally, I tend to like *The Ignatius Catholic Study Bible* for the New Testament and the *Jewish Study Bible* for the Old Testament. For a single-volume study bible, I like the *New Oxford Annotated Bible*.

Chapter 14: How to Discern

1. Timothy Radcliffe, *What Is the Point of Being a Christian?* (London: Burns & Oates, 2005), 198.

Chapter 15: How to Sustain Friendships

1. Jennifer Senior, "It's Your Friends Who Break Your Heart," *The Atlantic* (March 2022). https://www.theatlantic.com/magazine/archive/2022/03/why-we-lose-friends-aging-happiness/621305/.

Chapter 16: How to Be Uncomfortable

1. Dorothy Day, *By Little and By Little: The Selected Writings of Dorothy Day*, ed. Robert Ellsberg (New York: Alfred A. Knopf, 1983), 110.

2. Ibid.

3. Ibid.

Chapter 17: How to Be Mentored

1. Dostoevsky, *The Brothers Karamazov*, 18. Because there are so many editions of this novel, and you might want to find this section in your own edition, it is in Part I, Book I, Chapter 4.

2. Ibid., 285 (Part II, Book VI, Chapter 1).

3. Ibid., 313–15 (Part II, Book VI, Chapter 3).

Chapter 19: How to Grieve

1. St. Augustine, *The Confessions of St. Augustine*, trans. John K. Ryan (New York: Image, 1960), 59 (Book IV.9).

2. This is all in Book IX of his *Confessions*.

Chapter 20: How to Find Joy

1. Beth Haile, "Reflections on a Terminal Diagnosis," *Catholic Moral Theology* (November 13, 2018) https://catholicmoraltheology.com/reflections-on-a-terminal-diagnosis/.

2. Beth Haile, "Why I Am Leaving My Other Full-Time Job," *Catholic Moral Theology* (February 28, 2014). https://catholicmoraltheology.com/why-i-am-leaving-my-other-full-time-job/.

3. Malcom Muggeridge, *Something Beautiful for God* (San Francisco: HarperOne, 2003), 52.

4. C. S. Lewis, *The Weight of Glory* (San Francisco: HarperOne, 2001), 26.

About the Author

Leonard J. DeLorenzo, Ph.D., is professor of the practice in the McGrath Institute for Church Life and Department of Theology at the University of Notre Dame. The award-winning author or editor of more than a dozen books, his previous titles with OSV include *Model of Faith: Reflecting on the Litany of Saint Joseph* and *A God Who Questions*. Leonard is the creator and host of the popular radio show and podcast *Church Life Today*, and he speaks across the country and around the world on topics such as character formation, the biblical imagination, parenting and faith formation, and the witness of the saints. Leonard and his wife, Lisa, are parents to six children in South Bend, Indiana. You can find him online at leonardjdelorenzo.com and subscribe to his weekly newsletter at bit.ly/lifesweetnesshope.

You might also like:

A God Who Questions
By Leonard J. DeLorenzo

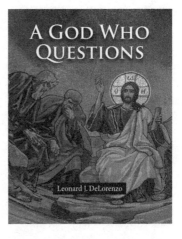

"Where are you?" God called out to the first couple in the Garden of Eden. He never stops asking us the same question.

The divine search for us continues in the person of Jesus Christ, the Word of God made flesh. When Jesus himself asks questions in the New Testament, he asks not because he needs an answer, but to draw us out of the shadows and into his presence.

This book examines twenty of the questions Jesus asks in the Gospels, showing us how they reveal the hidden secrets of our hearts and invite a true encounter with God.

You might also like:

Model of Faith:
Reflecting on the Litany of Saint Joseph
By Leonard J. DeLorenzo

The Litany of Saint Joseph is a powerful prayer that leads us to consider
the many ways in which Joseph faithfully
and diligently carried out the will of God.
As the litany guides us in proclaiming the
wonders of Saint Joseph, we are drawn
into contemplating the mysteries of God,
whom Joseph never fails to praise and
serve.

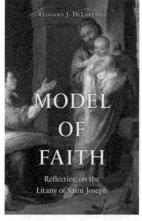

Each of the reflections in this devo-
tional focuses on one of the twenty-two
names, titles, or honors of Saint Joseph
that we encounter in his litany. As we pray to Saint Joseph, offering
our petitions to his care, and contemplating his life and his witness,
we are drawn into communion with God.

Available at
OSVCatholicBookstore.com
or wherever books are sold

Model of Virtue:
Reflecting on the Litany of Saint Joseph